Southern Literary Studies
Louis D. Rubin, Jr., Editor

A SOUTHERN RENASCENCE MAN

A SOUTHERN

ENASCENCE MAN

VIEWS OF
ROBERT PENN
WARREN

by Thomas L. Connelly,

Louis D. Rubin, Jr., Madison Jones,

Harold Bloom, and James Dickey

Edited by WALTER B. EDGAR

Louisiana State University Press
Baton Rouge and London

Designer: Albert Crochet
Typeface: Linotron Aster
Typesetter: G & S Typesetters
Printer and Binder: Vail-Ballou Press, Inc.

LIBRARY OF CONGRESS CATALOGING IN PUBLICATION DATA

Main entry under title:

A Southern renascence man.

(Southern literary studies)
Includes index.
1. Warren, Robert Penn, 1905–   —Criticism and
interpretation—Addresses, essays, lectures.
I. Connelly, Thomas Lawrence. II. Edgar, Walter B.,
1943–   . III. Series.
PS3545.A748Z868   1984   813'.52   83-14922
ISBN 0-8071-1138-4

Grateful acknowledgment is made to Random House, Inc.,
for permission to quote from the copyrighted works
of Robert Penn Warren.

"Under Buzzards," copyright © 1983 by James Dickey, is
reprinted from *The Eye-Beaters, Blood, Victory, Madness,
Buckhead, and Mercy* in *The Central Motion: Poems 1968–
1979*, by permission of Wesleyan University Press.

Frontispiece photograph by Mark Morrow of the University
of South Carolina

for ROBERT PENN WARREN
Southern gentleman, critic, historian,
novelist, poet

Contents

Preface

In July, 1980, the University of South Carolina decided to reorganize and expand the scope of its Southern Studies program. With the approval of the South Carolina Commission on Higher Education, an Institute for Southern Studies was created at the university with the threefold mission of encouraging undergraduate course work, supporting and promoting graduate and postgraduate research, and making public programs available to the greater South Carolina community. The institute was to be truly interdisciplinary in nature, not just for the study of literature. And, Southern Studies was to cooperate and coordinate its activities with other units on campus. The Institute for Southern Studies has remained true to its purpose.

Shortly after the reorganization took place, members of the institute's staff began discussing the possibility of a major public program that would underscore the interdisciplinary nature of the new Southern Studies program and would appeal to a lay as well as an academic audience. Almost immediately, the name of Robert Penn Warren began to dominate the conversation. Here was a man whose career of sixty years represented exactly the focus for which we were searching.

As poet, literary critic, novelist, and historian, Robert Penn Warren's versatility would enable us to assemble a diverse group of scholars for a two-day program. Carlisle Floyd's transformation of *All the King's Men* into the opera *Willie Stark* provided a unique opportunity to make the program even more interdisciplinary in nature.

In consultation with professors Ashley Brown and George

Geckle of the English department and John McCardell of the history department, a tentative list was made of those scholars who not only would be able to discuss a particular aspect of Warren's career but who could do it for the audience for which we were aiming. In addition, we were seeking scholars whose remarks would read well in essay form.

Given the scope of the planned program, Mr. Warren was contacted and he readily agreed to come to Columbia the last weekend in February, 1982. With his acceptance in hand, we began contacting the scholars for the program. The responses were immediate and enthusiastic. In addition to the formal papers on Warren's works, Carlisle Floyd agreed to attend and discuss the transformation of *All the King's Men* into *Willie Stark*. He also made arrangements for showing the major scenes from the television version of the opera.

With the program's lineup confirmed, the staff turned to the logistical and administrative details that a program of this size naturally breeds. All seemed in readiness when a letter from Warren arrived saying that regretfully he would not be able to attend the program. This was a blow, but not a single participant wished to back out. All wanted to continue. As Harold Bloom said, "We must. This is too important."

Originally, Warren had been scheduled to conclude the program on the second day with a reading of his poetry. James Dickey, who had agreed to introduce Warren, was asked if he would extend his introduction and read Warren's poetry in his absence. This arrangement was made upon the suggestion of Harold Bloom and with Warren's concurrence. Dickey graciously stepped into the breach.

In corresponding with Warren after his withdrawal, it was suggested that a video taped interview with him would be a welcome addition to the program. He consented and on the ninth of February, three members of the institute's staff with a crew from the university's Department of Media Arts flew to New Haven for the interview on the tenth.

As preparation for the interview, Mr. Warren suggested that Tom Connelly, Thorne Compton, and I meet him at Mory's for lunch. There, in a bastion of New England Yankeedom, four southerners discussed their Civil War ancestors, the splendor of Mobile in spring, and Jim Dickey's poetry. The leisurely meal was over all too soon and it was off to the Yale studios for the taping session. In later correspondence, Warren wrote: "I enjoyed our talk very much, until we got to the microphone. At that moment, darkness descends. I feel you came a long way for mighty little." With characteristic modesty, Warren understated his case.

The interview, conducted on camera by Tom Connelly, went well. Initally, we thought that we'd tape about thirty minutes and edit that down to a twenty-minute cassette. After forty minutes the flow of the conversation was going so well that taping continued for another twenty. The final version of the tape, edited by the university's skilled faculty from Media Arts, ran for approximately an hour. Connelly and Warren covered a wide range of topics from Warren's childhood in Guthrie, Kentucky, to his Vanderbilt years, to how he first began to appreciate and learn about his native region.

The essays appearing in this book are the papers that were presented at the University of South Carolina on February 26 and 27, 1982. The interview with Warren is an edited transcription of the video taped interview.

Friday, February 26, started off as a raw, nasty gray Carolina day. At 10:00 A.M., four hours before the program was to begin, Columbia experienced its second snowfall of the season. Although the meteorologists kept insisting that the snow would turn to rain, it did not. Hazardous roads and travelers' warnings closed many of the state's highways.

Despite the weather, which was more typical of New Haven than Columbia, folks by the hundreds turned out for all sessions. Students, faculty, townspeople, and out-of-state scholars such as Jim Justus came to listen and participate.

The Friday afternoon schedule led off with Connelly, followed by Rubin and Jones. Although each of these papers seems to provide a natural lead-in for the others, there was no advance collaboration among the authors. Each of the essays was prepared as an entity, but their common theme gives them a great deal of unity.

ROBERT PENN WARREN, A PUBLIC PROGRAM achieved what we had hoped it would. It was a cooperative venture involving the institute, the College of Humanities and Social Sciences, the departments of English, history, and media arts, and the Student Government Association. It was especially gratifying to all of us that the students of the university through their Student Government Association appropriated monies that helped make the program possible. Individuals whose cooperation and assistance made this program a reality were Nancy Vance Ashmore, Chester W. Bain, Elizabeth D. Bates, Barbara Bellows, Francis T. Borkowski, Ashley Brown, Matthew J. Bruccolli, Thorne Compton, Carey Crantford, Joan Davis, Carmine D'Alessandro, Elizabeth G. Edgar, Katherine Edwards, George Geckle, Donald Gray, Daniel W. Hollis, Larry Hudson, Thomas Johnson, Winifred King, Porter McLaurin, William Mould, Davy-Jo Ridge, Governor and Mrs. Richard Riley, Lori Shaw, Mark Spagnola, John G. Sproat, and Steve Wise.

Walter B. Edgar
Institute for Southern Studies
University of South Carolina

A SOUTHERN RENASCENCE MAN

Robert Penn Warren as Historian

His breadth and knowledge of southern—and human—understanding reaches back through sixty years in American letters.
He has achieved the goal of acclaim for the trilogy of poetry,
fiction, and criticism. Such work has gained an array of mer-
its—three Pulitzer Prizes for poetry and fiction, a National Book
Award, and many other honors.

In contrast, the labors of Robert Penn Warren in academic
history—the realm of footnotes and bibliography—are marginal. True, his first book *John Brown: The Making of a Martyr*,
was a historical work, but as reviewers noted, it was also a
literary biography. Then, one could mention Warren's two books
on the enduring racial turmoil in America; the review essays of
historical works such as Edmund Wilson's *Patriotic Gore*; popular magazine articles on Daniel Boone and the Alamo; his literary essay on the meaning of the North-South conflict, *The
Legacy of the Civil War*, and others. Some of these writings, such
as *Segregation*, his essay on Edmund Wilson, and *The Legacy of
the Civil War* are extremely valuable. But they would fall short
of the academic purist's conception of a historian.

Ironically, Robert Penn Warren is very much a historian, if
this means that he employs a philosophy of history and uses
past experience as a central theme. History *is* the thematic core
of all of his writing. It is the great dichotomy—history, the
blind force capable of human destruction, but also the salvation
of one who seeks self-identity. For Warren, self-understanding
comes through the application of the "historical sense." Self-
knowledge is the attainment of balance—between awareness of

1

self and the universal human nature, or between the mythology of the past and the realities of the present.[1]

This, of course, underlay Warren's famous essay on Samuel Taylor Coleridge and the "Rime of the Ancient Mariner," as Professor James Justus has reminded us. Warren, in "A Poem of Pure Imagination: An Experiment in Reading," suggested that form and content in a poem (idea and subject) should join to reconcile past mythology with present awareness. Both performed the task that underlines Warren's writing, in that moral sense is achieved from the wisdom of past experience.[2]

Always Warren believes there is the vital relationship between poetry and history, and the burden to reconcile the surface differences between fact and idea. "Historical sense and poetic should not, in the end, be contradictory," he observed in the foreword to *Brother to Dragons*.[3] The poet's burden—as that of the novelist—is to make sense out of the burden of time.

Here is the essence of the task of a discussion of Warren as historian. The tensions produced by the struggle between past and present underlie Warren's literary effort. The symbolism often differs. In a poem written as a Vanderbilt undergraduate, "Easter Morning: Crosby Junction," the confrontation came between the Resurrection pronouncements of the country preacher juxtaposed against "the confutation of the stone that

1. My understanding of Warren's philosophical approach to history is indebted heavily to L. Hugh Moore, Jr., *Robert Penn Warren and History: "The Big Myth We Live"* (The Hague, 1970); William C. Havard, "The Burden of the Literary Mind: Some Meditations on Robert Penn Warren as Historian," in John Lewis Longley, Jr. (ed.), *Robert Penn Warren: A Collection of Critical Essays* (New York, 1965); and James H. Justus, *The Achievement of Robert Penn Warren* (Baton Rouge, 1981). Other important material can be found in summaries such as Leonard Casper, *Robert Penn Warren: The Dark and Bloody Ground* (Seattle, 1960); Louise Y. Gossett, *Violence in Recent Southern Fiction* (Durham, N.C., 1965); and John L. Stewart, "Robert Penn Warren and the Knot of History," *ELH*, XXVI (March, 1959), 102–36.
2. Justus, *The Achievement of Robert Penn Warren*, 121–23; see also 25, 37.
3. Robert Penn Warren, *Brother to Dragons: A Tale in Verse and Voices* (New York, 1953), xii.

in the churchyard marks the mortal bone."[4] The quest for understanding came in "History Among the Rocks," part of a
longer narrative published in 1927 as "Kentucky Mountain
Farm." "There are many ways to die / Here among the rocks in
any weather," said the poet—die by the winter wind "down the
eastern gap," or by the "copperhead, / Fanged as the sunlight,
hearing the reaper's feet." One could die as well by the refusal
to accept history as a synthesis of the idea and the fact. So
rested once here the "gray coats, blue coats," young men "Blood
on their black mustaches in moonlight," destroyed by tragic
refusal to cope in their own ways, with the wisdom of the past.[5]
By 1929 poetry had become biography, but the theme remained
unchanged. *John Brown: The Making of a Martyr* was the story
of one who attempted to force history into a narrow pattern of
abstract idealism—who failed to oppose history with his human qualities but retreated into a concept of perfection.

Self-destruction or disillusionment comes because man does
not come to terms with historical experience. Thomas Jefferson
in *Brother to Dragons* overlooks the real human past and clings
to the concept of man's perfectable nature. The protagonists of
the twin poems "Bear Track Plantation: Shortly after Shiloh"
and "Harvard '61: Battle of Fatigue" demonstrate this potential
dichotomy in man. The yellow-toothed rebel soldier's view of
life is tinged with a deterministic cynicism, expressed as "Two
things a man's built for, killing and you-know-what." Now he
dies in anger because Jefferson Davis had promised that he
would slay ten Yankees and "hell, three's all I got . . . 'Taint
fair." The young New England soldier also lay dying. His self-
righteous moral idealism was no better than the enemy's coarse
view of life. He died in the blind faith that he was the better
man who would sleep "Beyond life's awful illogic and the

4. *The Fugitive*, IV (June, 1925), 33.
5. Robert Penn Warren, *Selected Poems: New and Old, 1923–1966* (New
York, 1966), 292.

world's stew. . . ."[6] The irony was, of course, that both men had failed to cope with "the world's stew." Like Adam Stanton and Willie Stark in *All the King's Men*, they had fought against history and had failed to cope with man's mixture of good and evil.

There were others who did grasp the dialectic between fact and idea. There was Adam Rosenzweig, the Bavarian Jew in *Wilderness*. His idealistic notions were countered by the real stench of the Civil War, but he kept his faith in mankind. Jed Tewksbury in *A Place to Come To* rejected his father—a symbol of the past—but escaped destruction in his quest for identity. His salvation was a symbolic return to a humble Alabama cemetery—a mark of reconciliation and awareness of complicity in the frail human endeavor.[7] Regardless of whether the character survives or perishes, tension is the central focus. All of these, Warren noted, were labors of "the terrible necessity of judgment."[8]

The point is, they also were what James Justus has described as "that grandest American dialectic." This was the clash of values between a Nathaniel Hawthorne and a Ralph Waldo Emerson—the eternal clash between a rugged Puritan insistence upon evil and a transcendental faith in man's goodness.[9] For Warren, this battle is fought in the context of history. Man's search for self-identity is complicated because he is burdened with a depraved nature. Despite Warren's denial of a religious heritage, his theme is undercut with faith in Original Sin. Here

6. *Ibid.*, 129, 131.
7. Havard, "The Burden of the Literary Mind," 181; see also Barnett Guttenberg, *Web of Being: The Novels of Robert Penn Warren* (Nashville, 1975), 104ff.
8. Robert Penn Warren, "Why Do We Read Fiction?" *Saturday Evening Post*, CCXXXV (October 20, 1962), 84; Moore, *Robert Penn Warren and History*, 53–55; Justus, *The Achievement of Robert Penn Warren*, 16, 11–24, 319–32; see also the editor's introduction to Richard Gray (ed.), *Robert Penn Warren: A Collection of Critical Essays* (Englewood Cliffs, N.J., 1980), 5, 3–11; important as well in establishing Warren's central theme is the same author's chapter in Richard Gray, *The Literature of Memory: Modern Writers of the American South* (Baltimore, 1977).
9. Justus, *The Achievement of Robert Penn Warren*, 329; see also 22, 330.

was the terror—a blinded individual cut loose in search of self-identity. The "terror of our condition" was the attempt to resolve order out of past experience. Hope comes if man accepts *complicity* in the human condition and understands that the mistakes of the son were also those of the father.[10]

This is no easy task. Even the best of Warren's fictional characters establishes a middle ground between idealism and reality only after intense suffering and participation in violence. Most fail to cope with the burden of time. Some reject change and retreat into the opiate of moral idealism. Others accept too easily the flow of evil in history, bend before the confusion of the past, and accept an animalistic determinism. True maturity, therefore, is the bonding of reality and ideal, past and present.

Warren sees this process as "the central tension in American literature." Here was the burden of the creative writer, he observed, because "historical sense and poetic sense should not . . . be contradictory." The interplay of subject and theme by the author must be a miniature world of the human quest for self-identity, in which the writer seeks "the true marriage of his convictions . . . with the concrete projection of experience." To Warren, the absolute goal is "reconciliation—that is what we all, in some depth of being want."[11]

The reconciliation is the climactic element in Warren's view of history and life. The struggle between moral idealism and reality within an individual must result in a synthesis—something sought by writer Warren as well as by his characters, whether John Brown or Jack Burden. The synthesis of self-understanding is an awareness of history. By understanding history, Warren does not mean merely taking historical facts and rising to generalize about human values. In his essay on Joseph

10. Moore, *Robert Penn Warren and History*, 64–65, 79–82; Gray (ed.), *Robert Penn Warren: A Collection of Critical Essays*, 2–3; Gossett, *Violence in Recent Southern Fiction*, 54.

11. Marshall Walker, "Robert Penn Warren: An Interview," *Journal of American Studies*, VIII (August, 1974), 234; Moore, *Robert Penn Warren and History*, 57; Warren, "Why Do We Read Fiction?" 84.

Conrad, he said the process was one in which "the image strives to rise to symbol." In brief, to understand the past, man must shape his own historical myth. As Warren admitted, myths were fiction, but fiction "which expresses a truth and affirms a value." Man can do nothing else. His grasp of the actual facts of history is feeble indeed. Little is known of the past, but self-understanding can come only when man makes sense of his heritage. So he creates a historical myth.[12]

The danger in guiding one's life by a historical myth is that one may shape a myth not based upon available facts. Warren's writing is filled with characters who endured tragedy because they chose to follow the wrong historical myth. Thomas Jefferson in *Brother to Dragons* follows a false image of human perfection. Willie Stark's myth of history was no better or worse—to him the past was an animalistic existence with "a lot of folks wrassling around." In *Circus in the Attic*, the United Daughters of the Confederacy's view of the Civil War became the repository "of ignorance as history." Meanwhile, in *Brother to Dragons* the Daughters of the American Revolution raised a monument to Thomas Jefferson's sister, Lucy Lewis, but the inscription "quite neglects her chiefest fame, that she / Gave suck to two black-hearted murderers." But, observed the poet, "let that pass, for to the pious mind / Our history's nothing if it's not refined."[13]

Still, the historical myth is essential to man's knowledge of himself and the past. It is the agent of synthesis—to unite the divided parts of man's inner nature. Warren's complicated philosophy of history and life dominates most of his writing. Whether a novel such as *All the King's Men*, a long poem such as *Brother to Dragons*, or a nonfiction work such as *The Legacy of*

12. Robert Penn Warren, "'The Great Mirage': Conrad and *Nostromo*," in *Selected Essays* (New York, 1958), 58.

13. See Moore, *Robert Penn Warren and History*, 125–41, for a full discussion of Warren's use of the historical myth; see also Warren, *Brother to Dragons*, 21.

the Civil War, there is this common element. They are all miniature worlds filled with tension between extremes of real and ideal, worlds where salvation can come through the historical myth.

Somewhere in Warren's own life between his birth in Guthrie, Kentucky, in 1905 and the publication of *John Brown* in 1929, he had fashioned this thematic approach to history. It appears first in *John Brown*—his first book; is glimpsed again in poetry and essays penned during the 1930s; is the theme of this first novel, *Night Rider* (1939), and thenceforth becomes his dominant theme.

Where did Warren obtain this approach? The search for anyone's source of inspiration involves risk. Still, one might suggest that in the first twenty-four years of his life, until *John Brown* was published, Warren lived in three situations which were in effect miniature worlds. All three were distinct periods of time that involved the interplay of ideals and reality and the emergence of historical myth.

First, there was his boyhood relationship to his Kentucky grandfather. By this I do *not* mean that Warren was a product of his own Kentucky upbringing. Some writers have overblown the image of Warren as a Kentuckian. His home at Guthrie lay just across the state line, in the rich oval of the Middle Tennessee bluegrass. More will be said of this later, but Warren was a child of Middle Tennessee—part of that intriguing social-cultural complex dominated by Nashville. "I always felt myself more a Tennesseean than a Kentuckian," he said.[14] Later, Kentucky certainly became a rich source of descriptive imagery in several of Warren's novels and a number of poems. But this was a cultivated trait—something that Warren acquired through actual research. The absolute border image of Kentucky—north and south, bluegrass plains and hard mountain rocks—would

14. Author's interview with Robert Penn Warren, Yale University, February 10, 1982.

become a useful metaphor. The grandfather was the central focus of Warren's Kentucky boyhood. Warren was never close to his own father, whom he described as "an intellectual who was more or less a failure as a businessman." Instead, he recalled, "my maternal grandfather was really more of a father to me than my own father was because I knew him better. . . . He was wonderful, an idol."[15]

His grandfather was also an absolute complex of the mythical and the real, his own miniature of paradoxes. Young Warren spent every summer in this world of southern dichotomies, and one could suggest that he learned three lessons filled with self-division. First, his grandfather represented those inscrutable paradoxes of the southern nature. He was a simple farmer who lived in a near-hermit existence, allowing none save the family on his lands. Yet he was, as Warren described him, a "bookish man" who quoted poetry constantly, and kindled his grandson's interest in the art. The grandfather was a voracious reader of history—Egyptian, Napoleonic, and American. On this remote farm, the old man possessed a universal view of the past much like the romantic historians in the era of Francis Parkman. The commonality of human experience, the overview of a broad landscape of the past—this Warren learned from his introduction to Buckle's *History of Civilization* and the writings of Prescott, Parkman, Motley, and others.

Strange it was that this man of letters had been a Confederate officer under the command of the semiliterate General Nathan Bedford Forrest. The memory of the war was part of this dichotomy between real and ideal. The *now* was the old farmer; the *then* was the war tales of a grandfather who raged larger than life, as part myth, part reality. He was Warren's first awareness of that southern self-division of alienation, the Con-

15. Carll Tucker, "Creators on Creating: Robert Penn Warren," *Saturday Review* (July, 1981), 38, 40.

federate and the American. His grandfather symbolized that absolute conflict in the values that brought the South to war. He was, as Warren said, "against slavery, but a good Confederate," who insisted that despite his beliefs on human bondage, "'I stand with my people.'" Here was that division between a southern code of ethics and a religion. The evangelical Dixie faith was grounded in metaphors of the goodness of Jesus, salvation and love for thy fellow man. The code of ethics was underlaid with stoicism—a pessimistic, almost deterministic philosophy which accepted failure and decline in a self-destructive manner. Disaster may come, but the important element was one's conduct—to "stand with my people."[16]

Probably the old man taught the boy also something about the essence of time as viewed by a southerner. The past is always within the present, and history is neither the *then* nor the past event, but is part of the *now*. Warren's poem "Court-Martial" declares this influence. The old man described how his company of Confederate cavalry had captured and executed some bushwhackers. The boy listened as "I sought, somehow, to untie / The knot of history." The vision came in the image of the execution, and of the old man, then young, riding away from the executed men still hanging from trees. The world is real. It is there. There because "the *done* and the *to-be-done* in that timelessness were one."[17]

Perhaps the old man provided a third inspiration. Warren's writing is filled with the imagery of father and son. In the quest for self-identity, the son revolts against the father, who symbolizes history or past experience. Wisdom comes only when the son, either literally or symbolically, returns to the father, to accept the commonality of human good and evil. Perhaps for

16. Peter Stiff, "An Interview with Robert Penn Warren," *Sewanee Review*, LXXXV (July–September, 1977), 467–68.
17. Warren, *Selected Poems: New and Old, 1923–1966*, 161, 164.

Warren, the publication of "Kentucky Mountain Farm" in 1927 symbolized his own return.[18]

By then, of course, he was away from the boyhood summers with the old man. In 1921, at the age of 16, Warren enrolled at Vanderbilt University. The subsequent years of his involvement with the Fugitive movement, the Vanderbilt Agrarians, and the total Southern Renascence has filled volumes.

Understand that Middle Tennessee had been always Warren's real world. Todd County, Kentucky, was part of that bluegrass oval—a complex of religious values, rich limestone soil, and paradoxes. Here Warren spent the first twenty years of his life. The chronology is recited easily. The freshman student in 1921 had intended to obtain a degree in chemical engineering. Soon he became involved heavily in literature, due to the influence of professors and fellow students such as John Crowe Ransom and Allen Tate. Warren especially became involved in poetry, and helped to organize the Verse Guild, which in 1923 published five of his poems in *Driftwood Flames*. That same year Warren became a member of the Fugitive Group—an informal body of Vanderbilt writers and local businessmen who met to discuss poetry. Warren left Vanderbilt in 1925 for graduate studies at Berkeley, Yale, and Oxford, but from a distance became involved with the Vanderbilt Agrarian movement in the 1930s.

From boyhood to involvement with the Agrarians, the core of Warren's real world was Middle Tennessee. Here was the essence of the theme of paradox that he would portray—of hope and reality, spirit and sin. There was an Edenic symbolism to the lush fields and green hills. Eden was also paradise lost. If anything characterized Warren's Nashville, it was tension. There was contradiction between the Old South and the new industrial order, and between the evangelical religion that dominated the countryside and the rising academic center at Vanderbilt.

18. See Justus, *The Achievement of Robert Penn Warren*, 11–24, for a full discussion of this theme.

The point is, that Middle Tennessee in Warren's era was a vast myth—a blend of the paradox of ideal and reality. There was the Confederate experience—with scarred trenches that remained in 1921 across suburban lawns and downtown churches that had served as field hospitals; but there was also New South boosterism and rising factory smoke. There was the imagery of life-as-myth in the palatial antebellum homes that dotted a map of the metropolitan area of Nashville, such as Belle Meade and Belmont; in nearby Franklin was the Valhalla of ancient cedars and weathered stones—1,500 markers to the dead on the bluegrass plain. Yet against this epic symbol was juxtaposed the seamy Ohio Valley river town, filled with wartime bordellos, which by 1863 felled 150 Yankee soldiers a day with social disease.

By Warren's time the interplay of tension was not between north and south, but between old and new, tradition and change. In the 1920s—even now—Nashville suffered from an identity crisis. Which cultural hat should it don? City fathers spoke proudly of the "Athens of the South" and pointed to Vanderbilt. But only in 1914 had the college won freedom from the control of Methodist bishops. Traditionalism endured on the campus, and some university officials even discouraged publication of *The Fugitive* magazine. Meanwhile, outside the university gates, evangelical faiths—particularly Methodist, Southern Baptist, and Church of Christ—laid siege to the school and the entire region.

Many of those who gathered at Vanderbilt in the 1920s or 1930s, in the Fugitive and Agrarian movements, had come out of such religious traditions in the rural bluegrass. Of course Warren espouses no formal religion and maintains he descended from a family of unbelievers. He protests too much. Warren's writing is enmeshed in the theme of Original Sin, and one is haunted by his remark in an interview, "I wish I were religious." Like Allen Tate in "Ode to the Confederate Dead," sometimes Warren resembles the watcher at the gate—caught up somewhere between the ideal of bluegrass evangelical faith and the reality of his own skepticism.[19]

Perhaps the Vanderbilt experience in part produced for Warren a synthesis between religion as ideal and fact—again, the establishment of mythology. Consider the influence of his tutor and mentor, John Crowe Ransom. As an undergraduate, Warren read Ransom's first book, *Poems About God*, which "opened my eyes to the fact of poetry in, even, the literal world." Soon came Ransom's poem "Armageddon" and finally in 1930, his influential book *God Without Thunder*.[20]

Ransom's influence upon Warren's approach to poetry has been well documented. Ransom taught that a poem was the creation of a miniature world. It was a constant interchange of content and technique, of facts and the author's form. More important here, Ransom's approach to poetry had religious overtones, which were summarized later in *God Without Thunder*. It was the writer's responsibility to establish religious myth in a world dominated by the pessimism and abstraction of science. Man needed the mythology of religion, even as a mere system of belief, in order to establish order amid change.

Of course Warren's Vanderbilt generation was indeed troubled by the search for order. Allen Tate's comment in his essay "The New Provincialism" has been repeated often. Here was a body of talented men gifted with what Tate described as "the backward glance"—a peculiar sense of perspective between Old and New Souths, between Confederate grandfathers and growing factory slums. Some, such as Ransom and Donald Davidson, had served in the Great War; or like Warren, some studied abroad and gained a perspective on the South in the total con-

---

19. Author's interview with Robert Penn Warren, Yale University, February 10, 1982; for a perceptive view of the cultural situation at Vanderbilt in Warren's time, see Louis D. Rubin, Jr., *The Wary Fugitives* (Baton Rouge, 1978), 1–10; see also John M. Bradbury, *The Fugitives: A Critical Account* (Chapel Hill, 1958), 3–27.

20. Robert Penn Warren, "John Crowe Ransom: Some Random Remarks," *Shenandoah*, XIV (Spring, 1963), 10.

text of Western civilization.[21] They searched for a system of truth in a world that placed faith in scientific abstracts or an idealistic notion of man's ability to progress. Their distrust of reason, science, and the abstract was influenced by a medley of authors—Chesterton, Eliot, Hobbes—even Saint Thomas Aquinas.

Louis Rubin observed in his book *The Wary Fugitives* that one should not dismiss the similarity between Warren's Vanderbilt group and the New England Transcendentalists. Obviously both attempted to create meaning from life in periods of rapid social-cultural upheaval. Both groups as well were caught between old religious values and new secular faith. The world of Ralph Waldo Emerson was one of talented writers, many refugees from Calvinism, who found little solace in the secular, business ethic of the Unitarian faith. Dispossessed between the ideal and the real, they sought their own mythology in transcendentalism and perfectionism.[22]

The Vanderbilt group would establish their own historical myth. In 1930, a body of poets, historians, novelists, and others issued *I'll Take My Stand: The South and the Agrarian Tradition.* So much has been written of the Agrarian movement that perhaps little remains to be said. We know these men were not advocates of a return to a rural past, but pled for a system of belief—belief in religion, in myth, in the objective system of truth. We know individual tastes varied. John Crowe Ransom, for example, spoke of the need for religious myths; Frank Owsley in "The Pillars of Agrarianism" was concerned with more practical economic and political issues. It is also well known that Warren had little formal relationship with the Agrarians. Studying at Yale and Oxford when the movement took shape in the late 1920s, his contributions to the canon were meager—a quasi defense of segregation titled "The Briar Patch" and a later essay, "Literature as a Symptom."

21. *Ibid.*; Rubin, *The Wary Fugitives,* 15–63.
22. Rubin, *The Wary Fugitives,* 3–6.

Still, Warren was very much an Agrarian, if Agrarianism is taken as a search for order out of the chaos of time and change. Like Ransom, Tate, and others, he sought to reconcile fact and idea into a system of belief. Warren's view was perhaps larger than the others, in that he was concerned more with the total human condition than with continuance of southern principles. Still, collectively, the search for order and myth in this group was affected deeply by the nature of culture in Middle Tennessee, which had been a montage of opposites—bluegrass farms and factories, evangelical religion and intellect, Todd County and Vanderbilt, the Scopes trial and H. L. Mencken.[23]

Warren's departure in 1925 for graduate studies at Berkeley was the last of the three acts of early life that shaped not only his view of history, but his craft of poetry and fiction. He recalled, "As soon as I *left* that world of Tennessee . . . I began to rethink the meaning . . . of the world I had actually been living in without considering it." He expressed a sense of alienation common to all southerners—a love-hate relationship with one's place and time. "The place I wanted to live, the place I thought was heaven for me . . . was Middle Tennessee . . . but I couldn't make it work," he recalled. He could not make it work because it was, but was not, his world anymore. "There was a time . . . when I considered going back permanently to Tennessee to live. I even got far enough to try to locate a place. I discovered the world had changed; it would have been artificial. . . . The world I'd be going back to would not be the one I was remembering."[24]

His vision was sharpened by the alienation of past and present, but Warren could not produce his own synthesis. "The South never crossed my mind except as an imaginative con-

---

23. For summaries of the Agrarian movement, see Thomas L. Connelly, "The Vanderbilt Agrarians: Time and Place in Southern Tradition," *Tennessee Historical Quarterly*, XXII (March, 1963), 22–37; John L. Stewart, *The Burden of Time* (Princeton, 1965); Rubin, *The Wary Fugitives*, 187–250.

24. Walker, "Robert Penn Warren: An Interview," 230; "The South: Distance and Change. A Conversation with Robert Penn Warren, William Styron and Louis D. Rubin, Jr.," in Louis D. Rubin, Jr. (ed.), *The American*

struct before I left it," he said. Now it became the focus of his philosophy of life and history. This was achieved by his own awareness of a partial entrapment in memory. Warren recalled once the first time he read a novel by William Faulkner. It was 1929, when "half of me was oriented toward Greenwich Village and the Left Bank and not toward the Cumberland Valley in Tennessee; but at the same time I was, I suppose, homesick." Henceforth, home for Warren became "a state of mind, a proper relationship to the world." He would describe the quest for such a relationship through an interplay of the reality of his own southern experience and philosophy of history.[25]

Out of this in 1929 came *John Brown: The Making of a Martyr.* Some critics consider the biography marginal at best, but it was an important book. It was the first full-blown evidence of Warren's philosophy of history which he would employ in later prose and poetry. It established the thematic pattern of his first novel *Night Rider* (1939), and subsequent novels such as *At Heaven's Gate*, *All the King's Men*, and *World Enough and Time*. It appears in *Brother to Dragons* (1953), in *Segregation: The Inner Conflict in the South* (1956), and elsewhere. The theme was self-division within one who searched for his own identity. Often he failed. Fed by idealism or determinism, one compromised with the world, justifying evil in the name of elimination of evil. Salvation—when it came—arose when one came to terms with his own complicity in history.

John Brown is important also because it established Warren's reliance upon the North-South conflict as a central focus. To Warren, the American Civil War was "the greatest single event in our history . . . our only felt history—history lived in the

South: Portrait of a Culture (Baton Rouge, 1979), 307; Richard Slade, "An Interview in New Haven with Robert Penn Warren," *Studies in the Novel*, II (Fall, 1970), 325.

25. "A Conversation with Robert Penn Warren, William Styron and Louis D. Rubin, Jr.," 310; "Intoduction: Faulkner: Past and Future," in Robert Penn Warren (ed.), *Faulkner: A Collection of Critical Essays* (Englewood Cliffs, N.J., 1966), 1; Slade, "An Interview in New Haven with Robert Penn Warren," 326.

national imagination." Here perished almost 620,000 Americans. Among them were one of every 19 white southerners, as compared to a loss of one of every 3,050 Americans in Vietnam. Human carnage was accompanied by millions of dollars lost in destruction and upheaval of every social, racial, political, and economic institution.

It was more than tragedy to Warren. It was the absolute metaphor of the American—and human—experience. Warren's book *The Legacy of the Civil War* (1961) is a metaphor of personal conflicts applied at the national level. Like a Jack Burden or a Jeremiah Beaumont, a raw, uncertain American groped for self-identity in the decades before Fort Sumter. Unable to come to terms with history or themselves, northerners chose idealism and the higher law; southerners embraced a pessimistic legalism which defended slavery. Both sides resorted to violence in the name of good. The catalyst of the war produced a search for mythology. Some of the myths were false—the South's Great Alibi, which disclaimed responsibility by virtue of being a captive of deterministic forces; and the North's Treasury of Virtue, a self-righteous approach which equally evaded responsibility. Somewhere in between was the synthesis of truth in historical myth. In the book, Warren never really establishes what this myth was supposed to be. He does suggest that one important synthesis to emerge from the Civil War was the advent of pragmatism, which did establish some working accord between ideal and fact. One might argue that Warren—and others who came out of the Renascence years—already had provided the *real* synthesis of mythology of the meaning of the Civil War. It was present, at least between the lines, in his book on the legacy.[26]

Perhaps it was the myth of the Lost Cause. How misused a term that is! Mention "Lost Cause" and one invokes images of

26. Havard, "The Burden of the Literary Mind," 186–92; Justus, *The Achievement of Robert Penn Warren*, 133–35.

aged rebel veterans in pitiful reunion camps; silver-haired ladies of the United Daughters of the Confederacy tenting on their own campground amid huge pastries and other desserts; or tan-legged majorettes at Ole Miss, tossing their silver batons to the strains of a brass band's "Dixie."

It was—and is—more than that. In an essay, Louis Rubin observed how ironic it was that no southern writer had produced the Great Confederate Novel. Even in the flowering years of the Southern Renascence, the talents of Warren, Faulkner, and others produced no *War and Peace*. In fact, Warren's Civil War novel *Wilderness* (1961) is centered upon a Union protagonist.

It was *not* the war—but the synthesis of defeat—that underlay the *real* Lost Cause. The Lost Cause was an acceptance of the reality of the meaning of defeat—of the extremes of the human condition and its self-division between good and evil, aspiration and reality. This has been Warren's theme. Southern mortals struggle in an American world that longs for perfection; the experience of failure is set against national belief in success. The South and the nation provided only the inspiration and the backdrop for Warren. The subject was humankind.

From the writing of *The Legacy of the Civil War*, the genius of Warren's ideas reached back somewhere—beyond his divided loyalties at Berkeley and Yale, even past the old battle trenches that lay around the Vanderbilt campus. Perhaps they went back to a time and place in those evenings on the solitary Kentucky farm, when a *real* grandfather told the boy stories about a mythical past.

The night finally came, but always the grandfather and the boy have been there in the morning.

Robert Penn Warren: Critic

Literary criticism, despite recent efforts to elevate it into equality with the literature it is criticizing, is essentially an ancillary activity. To the extent that it calls attention to itself rather than to the work of art, it fails in what it is meant to do.

So much, admittedly, is an assumption, based on premises that no right-thinking structuralist critic would grant, and today structuralists, post-structuralists and deconstructionists are riding high. It is, however, my assumption, and I assume it is also Robert Penn Warren's, as when he declares in his essay on "The Rime of the Ancient Mariner" that "a poem works immediately upon us when we are ready for it. And it may require the mediation of a great deal of critical activity by ourselves and by others before we are ready. And for the greater works we are never fully ready. That is why criticism is a never-ending process."[1] In other words, the purpose of literary criticism is to enable us to experience the work of literature with greater richness and depth than might otherwise be possible.

As I understand it, the theory of structuralism would have it that the poem or the story, having no identity beyond that of a system of signs, can have no existence except insofar as the signs are decoded by the reader. What the reader does, therefore, is to give existence to the work by making it his own work: he breaks down the system of signs and reconstructs it in order to display its functions. To the verbal object that is the work, he

1. Robert Penn Warren, "A Poem of Pure Imagination: An Experiment in Reading," in *Selected Essays* (New York, 1958), 271.

19

adds intellect; the result is a simulacrum, in which the functions are made intelligible.

Everyman is therefore his own poet, his own novelist; and since there is no check upon the activity of the reader doing the structuring, in the form of a text that must be deferred to, the structuralist critic is the virtuoso, playing word games, after the manner of the juggler keeping as many balls as possible in motion simultaneously: "Look, ma, no hands!" The critic is thus equally the creator; the only restraint upon his virtuosity is his own imagination.

If certain premises about the nature of language are granted, there is some logic to this way of looking at what the act of criticism involves. But it has its dangers. It can tempt the critic into a display of pride. Since the critic no longer explicates the poem or story, but rather thinks in terms of creating it for himself, he is encouraged to downgrade the poet's or the novelist's imagination in favor of his own. Pride, as we know, goeth before a fall; and the prideful critic, inflated with the brilliance of his own virtuosity, may find himself taking on a good poet or novelist on a one-on-one basis, and end up executing a pratfall in full public view.

We find this nowhere more perfectly illustrated than in the late Roland Barthes' *S/Z*, in which that performing Frenchman set out to develop his own simulacrum around and alongside the text of a story by Balzac. Dazzling and provocative though Barthes' verbal pyrotechnics were, it was a strategic error of crippling proportions, because he was up against a first-rate storyteller telling a tale. It was not very long, therefore, before I found myself skimming through Barthes' speculations in order to get to the next paragraphs of Balzac's text, so that I could find out what happened next. The "writerly" experience of Barthes at work on Balzac engaged my imagination so much less compellingly and vividly than the formal "readerly" experience of Balzac's story that it was only after I had finished the story that I was willing to go back to what Barthes was saying with sufficient patience to follow his commentary. Moreover, when I did I was both disappointed and annoyed, because the specificity of Balzac's text was so firmly in my mind that what I wanted from the critic was more help with understanding the reality of the literary experience I had just enjoyed, and not self-conscious demonstrations of his virtuosity. What I wanted, in short, was explication: a close reading of Balzac's text by someone skilled in literary analysis.

So much, then, for Geoffrey Hartman's assertion that literary exegesis is the "whore of Babylon," impoverishing our experience of the work of literature; what I needed at that moment was just such whoring.[2] I wanted a good critic to help me recognize the implications of what had been the powerful, intuitive immediacy of an engagement with a work of literature. A good literary critic could do that for me, because however much we might differ in our personalities and thus our personal responses to the story, it was Balzac's text that would dictate the terms on which both our responses took place.

I go into all this because Robert Penn Warren's kind of literary criticism is supposedly passé nowadays, and the textbook he edited with Cleanth Brooks, *Understanding Poetry*, occupies approximately the same place in the structuralist canon as the economic theories of John Maynard Keynes do in the Reagan administration. And this is as it should be, for the fundamental premise of the New Criticism, whatever its wide variety of approaches to literature, is that the essential job of the critic is to prepare us to read the poem, whereas that of structuralism is that this not only shouldn't but can't be done, and that what the critic perforce does is to recreate the poem in his own image. It is an important difference, because your working New Critic willingly and by conviction subordinates his personality to the

---

2. Geoffrey H. Hartman, "Beyond Formalism," in *Beyond Formalism: Literary Essays, 1958–1970* (New Haven, 1970), 56.

authority of the poem he is reading, preferring to let the text of the poem itself authenticate the terms of his response, while the structuralist views that as an unwarranted limitation on his own experience, and he grants no such authority—or author - ity as he might put it—to those verbal signs on the printed page. The choice is between humility and arrogance. Needless to say, I prefer the former.

It is scarcely an accident that not only Mr. Warren but many of the other leading figures among the New Critics of the 1930s and 1940s and 1950s were and are themselves poets and some-times novelists as well as critics, while to my knowledge none of the leading proponents of structuralism is thus inclined. If one writes poetry or fiction oneself, there is relatively little in-centive to want to claim for criticism a priority with the work of art it criticizes, and every inclination to let it remain an activity designed to help make the poem or story available to the reader. With the structuralists no such inhibition exists. The literary work, they declare, enjoys no privileged status as discourse; it is *écriture*, and so are critical essays, letters, political manifestos, and whatever. Presumably the difference between, say, "The Rime of the Ancient Mariner" and the *Biographia Literaria* is in degree of resonance only.

Without going very far into the semiotics and, I think, politics that lie behind this approach, I am constrained to note that if it opens up the supposedly closed system of the unitary poem to the freedom of intertextuality, self-reference, and participation in function, it also serves to elevate the critic into a position of creative status coexistent with that of the poet or novelist. Espe-cially if you are an English professor, this is rather nice.

It is also very democratic and free from any tendency toward class snobbery, in which instance—I quote Mr. Terence Hawkes —it is most unlike the New Criticism, which prizes such things as "sophistication, wit, poise," the stances "of a decaying aris-tocracy characteristically revered by a sycophantic middle-class" and emblematic of "a bourgeois mistrust of singlemindedness and commitment."[3] It you are a dominie at an effete institution patronized largely by the children of the rich, this too is very nice.

Because Mr. Warren has published a great deal of poetry and fiction, he need have no fears for his creative status; that much at least is assured him. As for his chances of avoiding the imputation of being a bourgeois, however, he would appear to be in deep trouble. For to repeat what Mr. Terence Hawkes has pointed out to us, the values of the New Criticism are based on "a bourgeois mistrust of singlemindedness and commitment," and if there is a single characteristic that Mr. Warren as critic tends to most admire in a work of literature, it is precisely its recognition of human complexity, its refusal to settle for singlemindedness, its awareness of mixed motives, modes, and responses.

Let me convict him with his own words. In his essay on "Pure and Impure Poetry," for example, we discover him praising certain writers—Proust, Eliot, Dreiser, and Faulkner—"because they have tried, within the limits of their gifts, to remain faithful to the complexities of the problems with which they are dealing, because they have refused to take the easy statement as solution, because they have tried to define the context in which, and the terms by which, faith and ideals must be earned."[4] Of Conrad's *Nostromo* we are informed that "nothing, however, is easy or certain. Man is precariously balanced in his humanity between the black inward abyss of himself and the black outward abyss of nature. What Conrad meant by and felt about man's perilous balance must already be clear, if I can make it clear at all."[5]

Mr. Warren commends Faulkner because that novelist "holds out no easy solutions for man's 'struggle toward the stars in the

3. Terence Hawkes, *Structuralism and Semiotics* (Berkeley, 1977), 155.
4. Warren, "Pure and Impure Poetry," in *Selected Essays*, 30–31.
5. Warren, "'The Great Mirage': Conrad and *Nostromo*," in *Selected Essays*, 55.

stepping-stones of his expiations,'" and for "giving a sense of the future, though as a future of struggle in working out that truth referred to in 'The Bear.'"[6] He admires Hemingway but is compelled to point out the narrowness of that writer's range: "We never see a story in which the issue involves the problem of definition of the scruple [of honor], nor do we ever see a story in which honor calls for a slow, grinding, day-to-day conquest of nagging difficulties. In other words, the idea is submitted to the test of a relatively small area of experience, to experience of a handpicked sort, and to characters of a limited range."[7] Katherine Anne Porter's irony is declared to imply "a refusal to accept the formula, the ready-made solution, the hand-me-down morality, the word for the spirit. It affirms, rather, the constant need for exercising discrimination, the arduous obligation of the intellect in the face of conflicting dogmas, the need for a dialectical approach to matters of definition, the need for exercising as much of the human faculty as possible."[8]

What such attitudes represent, we now know, is a barely covert elitism on the part of Mr. Warren. His belief in the complexity of experience and the difficulty of moral judgment is thoroughly middle class. I again cite Mr. Hawkes in mostly approving exposition of Barthes and others: "Thus, New Criticism's admiration of complexity, balance, poise and tension could be said to sustain the characteristic bourgeois concern for a 'fixed' and established, unchanging reality, because it disparages forceful, consistent and direct action."[9] He goes on to point out the insidiousness of all this, how the New Criticism corrupts the young: "The attitudes implicit in New Criticism itself may, in turn, be said to have been influential on the 'real foundations.' How many, one wonders, of the civil servants, the teachers, the journalists who generate the climate of opinion

6. Warren, "William Faulkner," in *Selected Essays*, 79.
7. Warren, "Ernest Hemingway," in *Selected Essays*, 117.
8. Warren, "Irony with a Center: Katherine Anne Porter," in *Selected Essays*, 155.
9. Hawkes, *Structuralism and Semiotics*, 155.

that ultimately shapes the actions of politicians and generals, derive at least some element in their total view of life from experiences whose essence is literary?"[10] Well might Mr. Hawkes declare, therefore, that from a Marxist perspective the New Criticism is "one of the ideological outgrowths of capitalism; dependent upon the 'real foundations' of its economic ordering of the world, and covertly reflecting and reinforcing these, while overtly it appears to address itself to quite other matters."[11]

Now if all this sounds familiar, there is a reason for it. It is the literary Marxism of the 1930s dressed up in semiotics, and what it is engaged in doing is not very different from what the comrades were doing back in the days of Christopher Caudwell, Mike Gold, Granville Hicks, and the Party line. That is, the assertion is that any work of literature, or way of reading works of literature, that doesn't contribute singlemindedly *to* the class struggle is *per se* lined up against the class struggle. Though the new code word is elitism rather than escapism, the premises— and the objectives—are similar. The New Critics are accused of having infected the young with their literary values of acquiescence in the capitalistic order. Their bland blunting of a single-minded commitment to social action, their belief in tolerance, their refusal to pass instant moral judgments, produced the war in Vietnam and other such civic delights, in exactly the same way that Marcel Proust caused the fall of France in 1940. In short, literature is at the barricades again, or at least criticism is, and what Winston Churchill once described as the "bloody-minded professors" are striving to show their militancy, for fear of being branded as lily-handed, superfluous intellectuals.

I do not know what Mr. Warren can do about this accusation. He may claim, as he does, that there is no such thing as a concerted critical movement known as the New Criticism: "Let's

10. *Ibid.*, 155–56.
11. *Ibid.*, 154–55.

name some of them—Richards, Eliot, Tate, Blackmur, Winters, Brooks, Leavis (I guess). How in God's name can you get that gang into the same bed? There's no bed big enough and no blanket would stay tucked."[12] But then he turns around and declares that "one thing that a lot of so-called New Critics had in common was a willingness to look long and hard at the literary object."[13] But to admit that is to imply the existence of the literary work, and that what a critic ought to do is to look at it long and hard, as if it were important *because* it is literary. It is to suggest that there is such a thing as a fixed text, the existence of which ought to control or at any rate guide our response to the story or poem, over and above what personal political, social, psychological, or economic assumptions we might bring to it. Mr. Warren's willingness to look long and hard at the poem even sounds like he favors that dread bourgeois activity known as explication. He appears to believe that we ought to use our intelligence, to the extent that we can, to develop a reading of the poem in terms of its own words, phrases, images, syntax, both single and as a totality, before going on to submit what it says to the test of its relevance to the "real life" experience about which it purports to comment. If so, then he is ignorant of the fact that, to quote Susan Sontag, "to interpret is to impoverish, to deplete the world—in order to set up a shadow world of 'meanings.'. . . Interpretation, based on the highly dubious theory that a work of art is composed of items of content, violates art."[14]

So there is no help for it: to the extent that Mr. Warren is a critic, he is a New Critic. The importance that he places on rendering the complexity of human experience, his belief that there is little in this world that is easy or certain, his assertion

12. "Warren on the Art of Fiction," interview with Ralph Ellison, in Floyd C. Watkins and John T. Hiers (eds.), *Robert Penn Warren Talking: Interviews, 1950–1978* (New York, 1980), 34.
13. *Ibid.*, 34.
14. Susan Sontag, "Against Interpretation," in *Against Interpretation and Other Essays* (New York, 1966), 7, 10.

of the constant need for exercising discrimination, and his un-willingness to jump at conclusions about one part of a poem without first testing them against other parts of the poem, make the indentification inescapable. Anyone who, in the course of discussing a poem by Robert Frost, could propose that "with our knowledge of the total poem, we can look back, too, at the next several lines and reread them" clearly deserves everything that he gets in the way of being accused of (in Ms. Sontag's for-mulation) depleting and impoverishing his experience through attempting to think about what it means.[15]

I exaggerate, perhaps—but only a little. One senses, behind so much of the convolutions of structuralist theory, the same impatience with "mere literature" that in the early 1930s sent the intellectuals fleeing toward the Finland Station. It turns up in strange ways. Geoffrey Hartman, for example, is no parlor Marxist and nobody's fool, but observe him in action, discuss-ing I. A. Richards' notion of literary form as serving to reconcile tensions and helping to unify discordant experience. "This theory is open," he says, "except for the very insistence upon unity or reconciliation, which has become a great shibboleth developed by the New Critics on the basis of Eliot and Rich-ards. . . . It is important not to be deceived by the sophisticated vagueness of such terms as 'unity,' 'complexity,' 'maturity,' and 'coherence,' which enter criticism at this point. They are code words shored up against the ruins. They express a highly neo-classical and acculturated attitude, a quiet nostalgia for the ordered life, and a secret recoil from aggressive ideologies, sub-stitute religions, and dogmatic concepts of order."[16] In other words, to say that one admires a poem because it has both complexity and unity, to praise it because even in its variety it is coherent and because the sensibility it exhibits is not that of an adolescent, signalizes a wish to avoid the discomforts and un-

15. Warren, "The Themes of Robert Frost," in *Selected Essays*, 130.
16. Hartman, "Toward Literary History," in *Beyond Formalism: Literary Essays, 1958–1970*, 365.

certainties of social change in favor of the *status quo ante* Sarajevo.

Thus when Mr. Warren declares of the "Rime of the Ancient Mariner" that it is a poem "in which the vital integration is of a high order, not one of the 'great, formless poems' which the Romantics are accused of writing," and asserts that his intention as a critic is "to demonstrate that the poem taken as a whole is meaningful," and says of Coleridge's poem, in terms of approval, that it is "in general, about the unity of mind and the final unity of values," what he is engaged in doing is exhibiting a quiet nostalgia for the ordered life.[17] Ripeness, in short, is not only *not* all; it is an elitist shibboleth.

It may be so, but I doubt it. The whole political analogy seems pretty sleazy to me. If we could take all the leading New Critics past and present and arrange them along the political spectrum, from left to right, I suspect, from the politics of those that I know, that the distribution would be fairly even all the way across. The history of American and English literature defies any such easy equation of attitudes toward openness of literary form with political allegiances. Whose notion of what a poem should be was more revolutionary in its time, that of the high church Tories Wordsworth and Coleridge, or the atheist-anarchist Shelley? Could there be any poet-critic whose literary views were more subversive of the fashionable middle-class notions of literary form in his day than the royalist T. S. Eliot? Wasn't it the Fascist Ezra Pound whose motto was "Make it New"? And when did either Eliot or Pound, as poets, show much concern for "balance" or "poise"? Allen Tate was politically a conservative; was he therefore, during his heyday in the 1920s and 1930s, a radical or a conservative force in his attitude toward the form and language of the poem? And so on; there is simply no reliable way to develop any meaningful correlation between a writer's or a critic's politics and his attitude toward

17. Warren, "A Poem of Pure Imagination," in *Selected Essays*, 266, 302, 253.

the preservation of the literary *status quo*, for the reason that the latter is customarily the product not of political but of literary history.

It is far more probable that the widespread discomfort with the New Criticism that has surfaced in recent years on the part of the structuralists and others, however ascribed to political and social outrage, is in actuality the inevitable manifestation of a change in literary generations. From the standpoint of the insurgents, what is really wrong with the New Criticism is not what Mr. Hawkes describes as its "bourgeois concern for a 'fixed' and established, unchanging reality," so much as the fact that it was developed and practiced by the academic literary generation immediately antecedent to that which is now engaged in attempting to run the show. In such a transaction the mere accession to power through orderly inheritance is never enough; what is demanded is repudiation. In any event, my own hunch is that when the smoke of critical battle subsides and Harkness Tower is securely occupied, it will turn out that what the structuralist critics on this side of the ocean do with a poem—as opposed to what they *say* they do with it—is remarkably similar to what the New Critics did. With the French, of course, it is another matter.

So much for the structuralist versus New Criticism dispute. What kind of a literary critic *is* Robert Penn Warren? He tells us that he is not a "professional critic," that a "real critic, like Cleanth Brooks or I. A. Richards, has a system—they develop a system," where he wishes to understand only this particular work or writer, and his criticism is a social activity in which he finds himself talking about books more or less as an extension of his teaching activities.[18] There is no reason to doubt this. I would only add that for a part-time activity pursued mainly for enjoyment and spare cash, his work has managed to be ex-

18. "A Conversation with Robert Penn Warren," interview with John Baker, in *Robert Penn Warren Talking*, 257; "Dick Cavett: An Interview with Robert Penn Warren," in *Robert Penn Warren Talking*, 287.

tremely influential insofar as the reading and teaching of poetry is concerned. *Understanding Poetry* completely revolutionized the way that poetry is taught in English and American colleges and secondary schools. Nor do I see any sign that its influence is receding; the structuralist controversy has not affected the basic way that a poem is now read and taught. The reason for this is that, structuralist polemics to the contrary notwithstanding, the abiding importance of the New Criticism is not as a theory but as a method, and it is Mr. Warren and Mr. Brooks who have developed that method.

It is a common assertion that the method of the New Criticism, as exemplified in *Understanding Poetry*, strips the poem of its history, ignores the personality of its author, and converts it into a meretricious verbal exercise. (I have seen Mr. Warren's colleague Cleanth Brooks criticised, in the course of a single polemic, both for being uninterested in the historical dimensions of literature and for conducting a covert apologia for the Old South, which is a pretty neat trick if you can bring it off.) Now anyone who possesses an acquaintance with Mr. Warren's work ought to know that, whatever else may be said of him, a lack of interest in history is not among his personal shortcomings. From the publication of his biography of John Brown in 1929 onward, he has been steeped in historical consciousness. To conceive of Robert Penn Warren without an abiding concern for the historical past is like trying to imagine a James Joyce who is unconcerned with Roman Catholicism, or a Laurence Sterne devoid of an interest in smutty stories.

What Mr. Warren and Mr. Brooks did do in *Understanding Poetry*, and did it very well indeed, was to establish the methodological principle that when you approach a poem the first thing you do is to read the poem. You look at the particular words and images the poet chose to use, and you do not jump to conclusions about what the poem means until after you have read it through and checked your response to any part of it against the rest of it. After that, whatever you do, in terms of history, biography, politics, psychology, theology, or whatever, is up to you. You can extend the poem's relationships to the world outside the poem just as far as you wish, subject only to the proviso that the ultimate place to look for corroboration of whatever you say about it is the language of the poem itself.

If this way of proceeding now seems very obvious, it wasn't when Mr. Warren and Mr. Brooks first published their anthology in 1938. Anyone who attended college during the 1920s, 1930s, 1940s, and even into the 1950s can remember courses in English or American literature in which the instructor talked about everything under the sun and moon except the actual words, images, and lines of the poem itself. When I studied Wordsworth in English Romantic poetry in 1942, I learned all about Annette Vallon, the French Revolution, Nature, the Lake Country, neo-Platonism and preexistence, Grasmere, Dorothy Wordsworth and Mary Hutchinson, and about emotion recollected in tranquillity, but when it came to the actual poems themselves, all that the teacher did was to read passages aloud in a husky voice and comment on the biographical or philosophical significance. Nowadays, thanks to Brooks and Warren, the equivalent of the same teacher will almost certainly begin, however mechanically or without imagination it may be, with the words and images themselves, so that whatever kind of pedantry or nonsense he or she might then proceed to pronounce, the students will at least have been exposed to what Wordsworth himself did in fact write. More than that, the fact that the teacher has been made to begin with the poem itself may serve as a checkrein on any impulse to stray too extravagantly far away from the poem under study, though this can by no means be guaranteed.

It has been charged that the method of the New Criticism, with its emphasis on close reading, places far too high a value on elements such as paradox, intricacy of image patterns, verbal wit, intellectual as opposed to emotional rigor, and so on, so that while it serves to show off the virtues of English Metaphysical poems and those of Eliot and his followers to good advantage, it is inherently biased against the Romantics and Victorians, and cannot properly uncover the strengths of poets such as Shelley or Walt Whitman. This seems dubious to me. It is quite true that Brooks and Warren, particularly in the early years of their collaboration, tended to admire the Metaphysicals and not to care for the Romantics, but there is little or nothing in the method itself that would establish any such favoritism. It is not in the close reading of the text, but in what is done once the text has been read, that Mr. Warren's—or anyone's—personal predilections come into play. The method itself, it seems to me, has no built-in bias at all, unless it is a bias in favor of reading what the poet actually wrote and taking it seriously. Mr. Warren himself has managed through close reading of texts to write sympathetically on Coleridge, Melville, Frost, and even John Greenleaf Whittier.

If we want to understand what Mr. Warren as a critic looks for in a poem or a story, we might examine the section of his introduction to Melville's poems in which he compares that poet's war poetry with Walt Whitman's. Though he begins with the flat assertion that "to my mind it is clear that Whitman is the bigger poet," it is obvious that Melville's poems interest him far more than Whitman's, for the reason, as he says, that Whitman's gift is for intensity and purity of feeling, while Melville's is for "complexity and painful richness of feeling."[19] Whitman, he says, is ritualistic in his war poems, while Melville is "dramatic, ultimately tragic."[20] He remarks of Melville that "his own yearning for absolutes—including, we shall assume, the absolute of Unionism—was modified by an agonizing awareness of the relativism of experience. The streak of mysticism in Melville was at war with his ferocious appetite to know. He was a mystic who hated mysticism."[21]

19. Robert Penn Warren, "Introduction," in Warren (ed.), *Selected Poems of Herman Melville: A Reader's Edition* (New York, 1970), 26.
20. *Ibid.*, 27.
21. *Ibid.*, 31.

It is precisely there, in that recognition of the potentially dramatic conflict between a desire for intellectual clarity and absolute consistency and a need to acknowledge the claims of the irrational, the material, the carnal, the contingent aspects of one's humanity, that Warren's engagement with works of literature customarily takes place, and it is to literary works that in one way or another focus on such a division that as critic he is drawn. Such words as *"yearning* for absolutes" and *"ferocious appetite* to know" are quite characteristic. It is no simple division of head and heart, intellect and emotion that is involved; the lure of the intellect, the desire for absolute knowledge, is perceived in terms of passionate emotional appeal. As critic he is quick to spot the presence of this opposition, and to develop its ramifications through close examination of the text. The conflicting demands cannot be left alone and ignored; an accommodation must be sought. The poem, the story therefore become arenas in which the rival claims strive to be reconciled in time, through action. Thus he says of Melville that what the Civil War "specifically did for him was to lead him to see that the fate of man is to affirm his manhood by action, even in the face of the difficulty of defining truth."[22]

Much of Warren's talent as a critic lies in his ability to search out and identify the lineaments of this dialectical conflict in terms of how they manifest themselves in and through literary technique: language, theme, form become dynamic elements rather than static entities. As critic what he does is to explore the workings of the division he has identified, extending his search throughout the texture of language and image and the structural development in time and action, tracing out the consistency of the development, and when encountering apparent contradiction attempting if possible to reconcile it. If it is impossible to do so, then he wants to know why. Thus of Thomas Wolfe's *Of Time and the River* he remarks of the characterization

22. *Ibid.,* 25.

of Francis Starwick that it "is more artificial, because he is at the same time a social symbol and a symbol for a purely private confusion of which the roots are never clear."[23] What he demands of a work of literature is internal consistency: its implications must be fully worked out.

By no means need this internal consistency be articulated on the level of conscious abstraction, however; where Mr. Warren looks for it most of all is in the imagery, the plot, the dramatic action. "The degree of consciousness in the creation of a poem," he says in connection with Coleridge, "is not necessarily relevant to its import: the real question is how fully, deeply—and veraciously because deeply—the poem renders the soul and the soul's experience, and thus enables us to understand it by living into its structure as projected in the structure of the poem. The only test of what . . . is 'latent' in a poem is the test of coherence."[24]

In Mr. Warren's instance, at least, nothing could be further off target than the claim, cited earlier, that what characterizes the New Criticism is its admiration for "complexity, balance, poise and tension" as devices for inhibiting change through disparagement of "forceful, consistent and direct action."[25] The recognition of complexity, the identification of difficulty are by no means sufficient; on the contrary, Mr. Warren again and again stresses, in his reading of a poem or a story, the absolute necessity for action. Knowledge must be put to the pragmatic test of being made to function in time. "But to live in any full sense," he says of Melville's war poetry, "demands the effort to comprehend this complexity of texture, this density and equivocalness of experience, and yet not forfeit the ability to act."[26] Discussing Frost's poem "Come In," he concludes that "so here we have

23. Warren, "A Note on the Hamlet of Thomas Wolfe," in *Selected Essays*, 174.
24. Warren, "A Poem of Pure Imagination," in *Selected Essays*, 281–82.
25. Hawkes, *Structuralism and Semiotics*, 155.
26. Warren, "Introduction," *Selected Poems of Herman Melville*, 22.

again the man-nature contrast (but we must remember that
nature is in man, too), the contrast between the two kinds of
beauty, and the idea that the reward, the dream, the ideal,
stems from action and not from surrender of action."[27] And so on.

What he does insist upon, however, is that the action be un-
dertaken with a full realization of its consequences. If, as Mr.
Terence Hawkes claims, "singlemindedness" is an object of
"bourgeois distrust," then Mr. Warren is thoroughly bourgeois.[28]
He is highly suspicious of self-proclaimed virtue; the literary
work that simply asserts and does not examine is not for him.
As critic he most assuredly does not value the poem that makes
easy, self-serving moral judgments, that does not question its
own premises or seek to avoid oversimplification. He declares
that "a poem, to be good, must earn itself. It is a motion toward
a point of rest, but if it is not a resisted action, it is motion of no
consequence."[29] Facile critical assumptions and pat formulas
are viewed with suspicion; "every new work," he writes in the
course of a discussion of Eudora Welty's early fiction, "is in
some degree, however modest, wrenching our definition, strain-
ing its seams, driving us back from the formalistic definition to
the principles on which the definition was based."[30] A critic who
can admire, and say why he admires, such divergent kinds of
poetry as Whittier's "Snow-Bound," the "Rime of the Ancient
Mariner," and Melville's "On the Slain Collegians," and fiction
ranging from Conrad to Faulkner to Theodore Dreiser, obviously
operates from no critical straitjacket. In James Justus' apt sum-
mation, "Warren's criticism finally reveals less the rigidities of
formalism, including the doctrine of autotelic art, than an older
notion of art as a complex function involving biography, history,
other art forms, religion, and psychology. Respect for the text is

27. Warren, "The Themes of Robert Frost," in *Selected Essays*, 127.
28. Hawkes, *Structuralism and Semiotics*, 155.
29. Warren, Pure and Impure Poetry," in *Selected Essays*, 27.
30. Warren, "Love and Separateness in Eudora Welty," in *Selected Essays*, 159.

not lessened thereby, but appreciates insofar as it is regarded as the product of a maker who is not aesthetic man only."[31] What being a New Critic means, so far as Warren is concerned, is that one starts with the text, and not that one is locked into it.

I hope it is obvious that in describing what Mr. Warren does as a critic, and what he looks for in the poem or story, I have also been describing what happens in his own poetry and fiction as well. The same sort of metaphysical dialectic between the lure of the idea and the exigencies of proud flesh that he discovers in the work he examines provides him with the dramatic situations that become stories and the occasions for often-anguished first-person meditation that lie at the basis of so much of his best poetry. It is his strength, and occasionally his weakness; when he goes wrong it is usually because he has attempted to force the kind of dialectic I have described upon a situation that will not sustain it throughout, so that he is led to try to get his point across by emotive rhetoric. But at its best, his work is made compellingly alive because of the way it breathes with the ardor of an urgent quest for human truth.

In an often-cited pronouncement made in the course of a critical analysis of Conrad's *Nostromo*, Mr. Warren declares that "the philosophical novelist, or poet, is one for whom the documentation of the world is constantly striving to rise to the level of generalization about values, for whom the image strives to rise to symbol, for whom images always fall into a dialectical configuration, for whom the urgency of experience, no matter how vividly and strongly experience may enchant, is the urgency to know the meaning of experience."[32] The passage has been frequently singled out as a description of his own poetry and fiction. What I would note now is the emotive quality of the words he ascribes to the effort to discover truth: "striving to

31. James H. Justus, *The Achievement of Robert Penn Warren* (Baton Rouge, 1981), 119.
32. Warren, "'The Great Mirage': Conrad and *Nostromo*," in *Selected Essays*, 58.

rise," "strives to rise," "the urgency of experience," "enchant," "urgency to know." The imagery is that of struggle, of compulsion. There is no room for complacency, no indulgence for efforts to take an easy way out. As critic of literature the work he customarily values is that which tests assumptions, uses language for purposes of exploration, seeks to leave nothing unexamined. In his essay on "Pure and Impure Poetry" he remarks characteristically that "nothing that is available in human experience is to be legislated out of poetry," and that "other things being equal, the greatness of a poet depends upon the extent of the area of experience which he can master poetically."[33] Again, the imagery is that of struggle. How anyone can describe the New Criticism, insofar as the work of the coauthor of *Understanding Poetry* is typical of it, as a conspiracy to propagate the notion of a fixed, unchanging reality is difficult to see.

It has been said of Mr. Warren's most recent verse that he has extended the range of his poetic experience to a remarkable degree, and this is quite true. The dialectic is still at work, however, whether in poetry, fiction, or criticism. Those who yearn for easy solutions, literary or otherwise, at whatever cost to intellectual integrity and moral honesty, had best look elsewhere than at Mr. Warren's writings for comfort. What he has to say as critic of literature is what he declared early on, in his essay on "Pure and Impure Poetry": "This method, however, will scarcely satisfy the mind which is hot for certainties; to that mind it will seem merely an index to lukewarmness, indecision, disunity, treason. The new theory of purity would purge out all complexities and all ironies and all self-criticism. And this theory will forget that the hand-me-down faith, the hand-me-down ideals, no matter what the professed content, is in the end not only meaningless but vicious. It is vicious because, as parody, it is the enemy of all faith."[34]

33. Warren, "Pure and Impure Poetry," in *Selected Essays*, 26–27.
34. *Ibid.*, 31.

Robert Penn Warren as Novelist

Three decades of criticism of Robert Penn Warren's fiction (and there is by now a great deal of this criticism) has still not produced very much in the way of a consensus. Such at least, from my brief sojourn among the critics, is the one clear impresson I derived—except, perhaps, the impression that critics as a whole are not a strikingly honest lot. Of course there are a few areas of general agreement, such as that Warren is a writer of great intellectual and imaginative powers, that *All the King's Men* is a fine novel and that the later novels are on the whole inferior to the early ones. But there remains an unsettling amount of butt-headed disagreement about which novels are good or bad and how good or bad they are and why. Naturally there is some of this kind of confusion in the case of every important writer, but it is especially true in Warren's case. The reason for this, I believe, is pretty clear. Warren's novels, for the most part, are unique, or perhaps peculiar, specimens of the genre. Freighted as they are with ideas, with meaning, they put strain on the novel form as we normally recognize it. Sometimes the strain is too much. But even in those instances in which Warren's adaptations are almost entirely successful, we are confronting rather a different kind of thing.

This statement is generally true of Warren's novels, but there is at least one exception. That one is his first novel, *Night Rider*, probably the only one of the ten that ought to be termed orthodox in character. It bears the mark of Warren's hand, all right. The impressive craftsmanship is evident, and the individual style, if not yet at its maturity, is developed in all essentials. But a still more striking mark of the Warren hand is the informing presence of the characteristic theme in its nearly full complexity. (Nearly but not quite full: this was to come only a little later.) It was the idea, the vision, which was to be the center of all his remaining fiction, around which all the novels were to form themselves as in a sort of ring. Now the work was exploration, the further definition and elaboration of this center. But already in *Night Rider* Warren was, to use the term he employed later in describing Joseph Conrad, a "philosophical novelist"— that is, "one for whom the documentation of the world is constantly striving to rise to the level of generalization about values."

Clearly the term "philosophical novelist" should not be taken to designate a breed apart, a class of novelists who like Camus or Sartre use the novel form, however skillfully and legitimately, as a vehicle for their ideas—or like Hawthorne, for that matter, as his notebooks indicate: "A man to swallow a small snake," Hawthorne writes, "and it to be a symbol of cherished sin." Here is an abstraction looking for an object to invest. But William Faulkner, who I perceive as having composed his novels in a way nearly opposite to the way of Camus and Sartre and Hawthorne, who distilled his meaning each time anew out of an image of raw experience, has just as much claim as these to the description. Degree of success is what justifies it: in their successes both kinds of novelists may rightly be termed philosophical. The difference, really apparent only to the extent that the novelist fails, is in the process. For the one kind, like Faulkner, the problem is likely to be in producing a coherence, and for the other kind, in producing too much of a coherence. It is a question of too much word or too much flesh. Either kind of excess will damage or destroy a novel.

Warren, I believe, belongs to that class of novelists who, when they fail, fail through excess of word, the self-conscious drive to produce meaning. This should not have been a surprise to one acquainted with Warren's uncommon intellectual powers, range of interest, and his moral passion. That novels written by him would be of a kind to cause some people to describe them, helpfully or not, as "intellectual" novels might have been forecast. In any case they all bear the burden of the author's determination to "mean." A few of them succumb all too fully to this determination. Some survive but go a little halt or become weakened by it. But there are the others, the ones that come to us as nearly unblemished as we have a right to ask of distinguishcd novels. These also may bear the marks characteristic of Warren's hand, but here they are manifested mainly in a uniqueness of the strategies by which word and flesh are made one.

The center, the clear thematic concern of all Warren's fiction, has been with what Jack Burden in *All the King's Men* calls "the terrible division of our age," modern man's failure to achieve wholeness or full identity. The novels dramatize consequences of this condition and the struggle, often unsuccessful, toward completion of self in the knowledge which is wholeness. Jack Burden, the novel's protagonist, is trapped in his state of "innocence," of denial and willed noninvolvement in the dark world of nature, of blank fact, which Willie Stark embraces. Jack's is an incomplete and therefore a false self, and his story is the story of his breaking through, after the carnage he makes, to a realization of his inescapable part in and responsibility for the world he has denied. He accepts the dark within and without, and thus defining himself in his limitations is able at last to enter the human community. Now he is whole, his existence is real, he is prepared to go "into the awful responsibility of time." This is Warren's secular version of the Christian scheme of redemption, in which, roughly, denial of limitations equates to pride, acceptance to humility, and wholeness achieved in the context of community, to salvation.[1]

---

1. For a helpful description of Warren's basic themes, see Barnett Guttenberg, *Web of Being* (Nashville, 1975).

Such, in essence, is Warren's theme, which perhaps achieves its fullest statement in *All the King's Men*. But to say this is not to say that the theme achieves here its most successful statement in dramatic terms. I think that it does not, and that the novel, for all its many excellences and its display of Warren's often astonishing powers, suffers from the same weakness that exists, to one degree or another, in most of his novels. It is a weakness that arises, perhaps, from the very richness and variety of Warren's intellectual and imaginative gifts, gifts that may present a difficulty which does not confront most skilled artists. The difficulty, I believe, is that of preserving in its full integrity the mode of thought peculiar to the practice of a certain art, in this case the art of fiction. Not that all of Warren's novels are in consequence damaged. I would almost entirely except *World Enough and Time* and *The Cave*, which are in a way special cases, and I would also except *Night Rider*. But I would bring the charge to bear generally on the other novels, not excluding the much-praised *All the King's Men*.

If it can be said that a novel is richer in meaning than in dramatic force, the statement expresses an unfavorable judgment of the success of the novel.[2] What the statement further tells us is that at least a part of that meaning is not of a kind which the novelist's art, at least as we normally understand it, can produce: it is another kind of meaning, appropriated from some other realm than the imaginative. It is a mixing of modes. The philosophic novelist is, to repeat, "one for whom the documentation of the world is constantly striving to rise to the level of generalization about values." And Warren adds, "For him the very act of composition [is] a way of knowing, a way of exploration." Warren at his best is a philosophic novelist. But too often he fails to evade the danger to which the species is subject in practice: allowing philosophy, or abstract meaning, too much

2. This essay makes extensive use of quotation from my essay "The Novels of Robert Penn Warren," *The South Atlantic Quarterly*, LXII (1963), 488–98.

voice in art. When this happens, the process described in the quotations above is reversed: generalization about values may strive toward documentation in the world, and the act of composition become a way not of knowing but of showing something. Art then ceases to be a way of thinking and its object tends to become the popularization of an idea, however serious the artist's ultimate intention. This is the weakness which Warren's novels do not always escape. It is what gives to certain of them their air of parables or morality plays.

All the King's Men is the story of Jack Burden's reorientation to life. "The end of man is to know," he says, and the novel is about how he comes from the womb-state of innocence to knowledge. It is Jack Burden's story, but Willie Stark, the Boss, man of stark fact who bends nature to his will—hence his name—early seizes the stage and indeed holds it for so long that some, more obtuse readers have remained confused as to who the real protagonist is. But this seems to be no problem for a long while. Well into the second half of the novel, with Jack Burden acting as a sort of neutral narrator-participant, the drama continues to mount in force. The inherent difficulty, signaled by a decline of dramatic power, becomes apparent only at that late point where Jack's strictly personal situation looms into the foreground of the action. It is, of course, part of the meaning that no human situation is strictly personal: "We eat a persimmon," says Jack, "and the teeth of a tinker in Tibet are set on edge." It is also true that Jack's personal situation has been with us all along and that it has been so prepared as to take its place in the pattern of action and meaning. What we are not prepared for is its usurping, at a late and crucial point, the dramatic focus. Until now, through Jack Burden, Willie Stark has been so forcefully placed at the center of interest that we cannot but be prepared for the crisis of Jack's personal dilemma to be enacted pretty directly, and dramatically, in terms of Willie's. Instead, however, two essentially distinct lines of action develop: the crises of Jack Burden and Willie Stark cease to draw real breath from one another, cease to relate palpably to each other as parts of a substantial dramatic whole.

Two-thirds of the way through the novel there comes the long summary chapter—comparatively undramatic—in which Jack gives us the story of his early relationship with Anne Stanton, a story that illuminates the state of willed innocence that has stunted him. Not many pages later—after an interval in which Willie's story is again the focus of interest—comes the episode in which Jack causes the death of Judge Irwin and then discovers, through his mother, that not the Scholarly Attorney but Judge Irwin was his actual father. This is the moment of Jack's rebirth: he bursts finally from the womb. "It was like the ice breaking up after a long winter," he says, and he is past the climax of his own story. If Jack is the protagonist—which he clearly is, since he is the one affected, educated, by the full sweep of the novel—then what comes after the climax of his personal story must be anticlimactic. But the great moment, the assassination of Willie Stark toward which the really dramatic interest of the novel has been building, is still to come. The effect is precisely anticlimactic.

It is not merely the structural split that diminishes Willie's thunder. We now have come, because of the episodes mentioned above, to take Jack Burden as true protagonist seriously; and since he has already burst out of his former condition of innocence, the assassination of Willie Stark by Adam Stanton cannot be for him the great climactic stroke of light—as it should dramatically—but only the earliest important one in a series of illuminations that come as he puts together his new vision of the world. He sees the meaning in the event—the man of pure fact and the man of pure idea are destined to destroy each other—but it is not this meaning which liberates him. His already achieved condition of freedom is the condition of his understanding, and the meaning is only an extension of the new vision developing in his mind. Well before the death of Willie Stark the novel has begun to deflate. Its greatest moment is partly dissipated by the refusal of the two stories—each an element in the author's pattern of ideas—to unite in a dramatic whole. And for final illustration of the point there is the leftover effect of the ending, in which Jack, with little dramatic context to support him, must go about completing the meaning for which the pattern calls. The flaw in *All the King's Men* thus originates in the author's determination to extend meaning beyond the limits that his material demands.

An analysis like the foregoing often seems to indicate that the writer is for good and all disposing of his subject. Let me hasten to deny that this is the case here. The novel clearly survives the flaw I have described. The fact that thirty-five years after publication it is still solidly with us says as much, and so, more convincingly, does the sheer abundance of the novel, which for me has affirmed itself through still another reading. The novel's great range, its subtlety and rhetorical brilliance, and above all its swarm of living human beings must give it substantial place not only in Warren's canon but in our recent literature.

Nevertheless the flaw is there. It is characteristic of Warren's novels and in several instances does a good deal more damage than is the case in *All the King's Men*. *Band of Angels* comes to mind. This novel, despite the author's enormous ingenuity and some brilliantly dramatic episodes, comes very near the appearance, especially in its latter part, of merely dramatized statement. The fundamental trouble is with the protagonist herself, Manty Starr, who is also the first-person narrator. She is not so much a person as she is the cooked-up bearer of a false condition that in the author's scheme of salvation is typical of our humanity. Manty is of mixed black and white blood, symbolical of the human plight, and her persistent denial of the black and therefore of the dark, the void, human limitation, traps her in the false self which is the world's natural victim. Convincing indication of this cooked-up quality of the novel appears in the early pages, in the initial improbability that Manty, in the bosom of her home community, surrounded by friends at the funeral of her father, could be hauled away thus brutally into slavery. This same neglect of the literal level results in creation of characters that are virtually pure caricatures—Seth Parton and Miss Idell (notice the names)—and in a slightness of character in such central figures as Tobias Sears and Rau-Ru. And as with *Bands of Angels*, so too (if by no means always this visibly) with other of the novels. In *Wilderness*, for instance, there is the protagonist Adam Rosenzweig with his emblematical crippled foot and corrective boot; and in *Meet Me in the Green Glen*, the damaging switch virtually in midstream of one protagonist for another. In the ascendancy of meaning, the flesh is bound to suffer.

But if Warren's novels pretty often suffer for this reason, the suffering is not fatal, for there are those novels that go virtually unscathed. These are *World Enough and Time* and *The Cave*, which I rate as major achievements, and also *Night Rider*, which, if not the equal of these two, is surely an impressive piece of work. *Night Rider* is of course Warren's first novel. It lacks the reach and abundance of Warren's work at its fullest maturity and leaves us finally, as the later works do not, with little sense of the affirmative possibilities inherent in the human condition. But the novel's very austerity is one of its beauties. And Warren has rarely been more subtle in tracing the psychological progress of a protagonist as he moves from mode to mode of false being, seeking to fill the void of himself with illusions of reality. We are not troubled here by a sense of characters situated or moved by an author's hand. And that scene in which the Night Riders gather and destroy the tobacco warehouses of Bardstown is perhaps the finest piece of sustained action in all of Warren's fiction.

But *World Enough and Time* is a work of Warren's full maturity. Like all works of great merit, the novel derived partly from an initial stroke of luck, or what seems like luck. Warren was shown the pamphlet describing the trial, in 1820, of Jereboam Beauchamp (Jeremiah Beaumont in the novel) for the killing of

Colonel Sharp. This was the seed, and given Warren's peculiar concerns and array of talents, it was something like the perfect seed for him. Here in essence was a fully expressive image of his theme, including elements that made it possible for him to unite a personal and private thing with a public thing. Technique is shaped by theme, and it can be seen in *World Enough and Time*, as in most of Warren's novels, how the technique employed answers to the psychic configurations of his theme. Warren's is a technique devised to join in a fictional wholeness elements that may seem disparate—analogous to the human effort to unify and heal division of the self. The technique is vital to Warren's art as novelist, just as the idea that shapes it is vital to his thought; and it is an important means by which he achieves the great range and relevance of his novels.

The use of the political issue in *World Enough and Time* is one of Warren's most brilliant variations on this technique. The Old Court–New Court conflict envelops the private story of Jeremiah Beaumont, and Jeremiah's very reluctant and short-lived participation in its struggles is index of that isolation or incompleteness of self which destroys him: his unwillingness is part of his rejection of the blemished world for the sake of the pure idea, to preserve what he considers to be his perfect integrity of self. But the presence in the novel of the political issue has far other purpose than simply this. The issue of Old Court versus New is one between the concept of law as absolute moral ruler to which man must yield and the concept of law as servant of man's needs.[3] The conflict is therefore extension and reflection of Jeremiah's inner conflict: the opposing political points of view are equated with the opposing points of view that succeed each other in Jeremiah's mind—that the idea should redeem the world and, then, that the world must redeem the idea. Just as New Court seeks to interpret at will the state constitution that it might serve an idea of justice, so does Jeremiah

3. Leonard Casper, *Robert Penn Warren: The Dark and Bloody Ground* (Seattle, 1960), 146.

take law into his own hands that justice might be done to Colonel Fort, whom Jeremiah murders. Jeremiah's second error—use of the world to redeem the idea—which grows out of the first, thus has its clear political parallel. The effect is to universalize the conflict within Jeremiah. And this effect is one with the implication that in the political story, in terms of Colonel Fort, lies the way to wholeness, which Jeremiah rejects finally with violence. Parenthetically it ought to be said also that the presence of the political parallel is one of the things that prevents Jeremiah's seeming a victim of mere eccentricity, an ever-present danger with such a protagonist.

So stated, the evident parallel between the public and the private issue may seem arbitrary, a yoking together. It is not. Such a flaw is prevented by the intricate dramatic interweaving of the two elements. Jeremiah's brief participation in the political conflict is one means of effecting this dramatic fusion. But more important is the fact that the two elements come together as one at the very center of the novel, the murder of Colonel Fort. Fort, father surrogate of Jeremiah, is very much a part of the world in which the political conflict is enacted: he is a man *of* this world, embodying the necessary spirit of humble accommodation which Jeremiah so contemns. On the night of his death Fort announces that he has a plan, to be revealed next morning, that will resolve the conflict between the factions. In murdering Fort, Jeremiah murders also the plan that would have reconciled the opposites. Intruding from out of his private world, he at one stroke destroys the possibility of reconciliation in public and private worlds alike. The political factions will go on fighting until one eliminates the other, perpetuating that imbalance which is injustice and which ravages the body politic. And privately in killing the father—symbolic of the human community, of tradition and responsibility to past and future—he has slain the spirit that could have made the only possible unity of world and idea in himself. Now, alienated from humanity by the ritual shedding of its blood, he has delivered himself up finally to the ravages of the pure and inhuman idea, which effects his destruction. The murder of Fort is a point of beautiful interaction between the private world of Jeremiah and the public world of Fort, and demonstrates the integrity of the whole. Jeremiah rejects, murders, what he must have—the community which is the word made flesh. Thus the public element of the novel dramatically illuminates, as well as projects, Jeremiah's very modern dilemma. And here as elsewhere in the novels we clearly see the extent to which Warren's view is the classic one, conceiving of the purely private self as incomplete, and of the community as analogue or projection of the individual.

The use in *World Enough and Time* of the anonymous historian-narrator brooding over the romantic account of Jeremiah Beaumont's career is perhaps Warren's most fortunate adaptation of his peculiar talents to the novel form. The narrator is of course, first of all, an indispensable part of the story. There are not a few moments when the motives generated by Jeremiah's romantic idealism approach, at least for a modern reader, the point of absurdity. But we have the narrator as mediator. He has warned us. "At times," the narrator says, "even he, the hero, forgot his lines. At times it all was only a farce . . . with its comic parody of greatness. . . . To us, at this distance . . . it is sometimes the most serious speeches and grand effects which give the farce." The narrator's authority, his gravity and sympathy, and the distancing his presence makes, are what holds the reader's response within the necessary limits. But the narrator's presence does more than this. He is himself a sort of participant in the story and, as such, through his questionings and his brooding meditations, he makes legitimate the concern with pure meaning in the novel. His presence makes possible the novel's rich compound of substance and meaning, to the end that the reader may be able, in Warren's words, to see "how idea is felt and how passion becomes idea through order."

But the foregoing gives only a poor idea of the richness and the range of *World Enough and Time*. Robert B. Heilman, in an excellent essay on the novel, details its many riches, pointing to, among other things, the diversity of motifs and patterns, the complex interrelationship of parts, and the various terms in which the book can be read.[4] Most interestingly, perhaps, he points to the novel's many literary analogies—with George Eliot, with Conrad, with Elizabethan drama, and with Shakespeare in particular, especially *Hamlet*. Like Hamlet, Jeremiah, the questioner, plots revenge, makes use of a literary mousetrap, declines to kill Fort when to do so would seem morally incomplete, abuses and drives his sweetheart to madness and, late in the novel, even listens to the quips of a gravedigger. There are these and more. If such as this is what prevents Warren from being a writer of "primary" fiction, as Maxwell Geismar once said, then we badly need to revise our estimate of writers like Joyce and T. S. Eliot.

But *World Enough and Time* has received at least in considerable part the praise it deserves. Not so *The Cave*. The reception that followed *The Cave's* publication in 1959 was, with a few honorable exceptions, one of incomprehension and, in some cases, disdain. The novel was charged with being slick, sensational, theme-ridden, and, conversely, with having no point at all to speak of. In the years since, there have been a few good essays about the novel, but nowhere near enough to inspire the recognition it ought to have. *The Cave* is a brilliant book. It is the most human, the most compassionate of Warren's novels. It is also the most unique.

I have made a point of the fact that all of Warren's novels center around a constant theme, that scheme of idea that is his secular version of the Christian scheme of salvation. In this respect the novels are uncommonly similar: as I have said, they form a sort of ring around a common center. What I have not pointed up is the extent to which they vary from each other in

4. Robert B. Heilman, "Tangled Web," in *Robert Penn Warren: A Collection of Critical Essays*, ed. John Lewis Longley, Jr. (New York, 1965), 96–109.

body, tone, and technique. From this perspective, not only are there no two novels that are alike: there are no two that even very closely resemble one another. The protagonists of the different books, for instance, are remarkably various in character, as radically different from each other as Perse Munn in *Night Rider* and Jed Tewksbury in *A Place to Come To*. Structurally each novel, employing a different central image, is designed to engage the theme from a new angle. And technical point of view ranges pretty well across the spectrum from simple first person to omniscient. So, although the theme is a constant, the variety of means by which the theme is engaged gives in each case a different experience of it. Of course this determination of the author to approach his theme each time in a new way puts some strain on the novel form as we recognize it. Sometimes, we may be tempted to say, they pass beyond the merely unique and barely are novels at all. In the case of *The Cave* this may partly explain the not very favorable reception and the relative limbo in which the novel has so far remained.

The Cave has no clear protagonist at all, though Jack Harrick, the aged and dying blacksmith, formerly Hell's own high-stepper, comes nearest to that role. Instead there are six major characters who share almost equally in the novel's focus, and another half dozen who are, each in his degree, lesser points of focus. Absent, therefore, is the kind of dramatic force naturally inherent where a novel's concentration rests on the story of a single character, or at least on the clearly related stories of only a very few characters. With the focus so scattered among so many diverse lives, how is the novelist to make a dramatic unity? This is the kind of question that the late poet E. E. Cummings might have asked himself. I ask it only to suggest, in the case of this novel and also of other of the novels, the relationship between Warren the novelist and Warren the poet.

In *The Cave* the question is answered in terms of the novel's central image—that of the cave itself and the young man trapped inside it—and the reflection of that image in the deep psychic and moral need of the novel's characters. As the young man in the cave is trapped, a prisoner (the novel's epigraph is from Plato's allegory), so is each one of the many characters trapped in the cave of himself, his own darkness or world of shadows that is his own false self. To be led out, educated, into the world of light is the need of every one, and necessarily involved is each one's recognition of his own entrapment and the causes that maintain it. This is the recognition of our human limits, of the flawed humanity we share with all men. Recognizing this, accepting the darkness within and without, we make possible community and love which generate the light. Without such recognition a life is stunted, and this stuntedness is the common predicament of the novel's many characters. It is also the predicament reflected in the cave image, which furnishes the center around which the novel turns and to which all the characters, for better or worse, are finally drawn.

This cave image is symbolic, of course, but it is symbolic in the full naturalist signification of the term. It is no emblem but a real cave with a real man, Jasper Harrick, trapped in it, and out of this man's physical predicament and his connection, direct or indirect, with all the characters, the novel's action stems. Starting with the discovery of Jasper's situation by his younger brother Monty and Monty's pregnant girl friend, the action moves on its slow circling course, gathering as it proceeds the many diverse participants into a unity that draws them all, reluctant or not, finally to the cave's mouth. Structurally at least, Warren never did anything more subtle. From personal situations that seem unbridgeably diverse, life after life flows or erupts into the general involvement, each one finding in the common crisis its own redemptive or destructive resolution. This is structure that might itself be called illustrative, figuring in the shape of the action Warren's idea of the inescapable, if unadmitted, unitedness of mankind.

It may appear from my description that *The Cave* would be the kind of novel just calculated to display that insistence upon

meaning which damages other of Warren's novels. So many
characters trapped in their own false identities might seem to
present a situation bound to produce the kind of repetitiveness
of treatment that too clearly shows the author's hand. But here
Warren's great ingenuity and his power with character quite
forestall the danger. There is no such repetitiousness: the personal crises and their resolutions are as many and individual as
there are characters to experience them. Isaac Sumpter, who
fails of redemption, whose ultimate fate is never to be more
than himself, confronts his own nothingness with the illusion of
power. He is the schemer, the puller of strings, victim of his own
manipulations. MacCarland Sumpter, Isaac's father who does
not fail of redemption, is frozen in the basilisk eye of his own
uncompromising theological commitment. Nick Pappy, the
Greek, in whose soul the tears fall without ceasing, is trapped in
a sort of Keatsian entrancement with the unobtainable vision.
And Jack Harrick, father of Monty and the trapped man in the
cave, lives not in his own proper life but in a legend of himself
that afflicts not only him but also his wife and sons. The common predicament of the other characters also is expressed in
forms as various as these. As various and, because they are the
stuff of daily life, as readily available to imagination.

Excepting *All the King's Men*, no other of Warren's novels
gives us an array of characters at once so diverse and so vividly
alive. I say this in the face of opinions that charge Warren here
with having created characters that verge on caricature. Although the reason behind the charge is clear enough, this is
essentially a misunderstanding. In the novel's scheme there are
characters who succeed and others who fail, those who escape
from their false selves and those who do not. The Greek, for
instance, is among those who succeed. Beginning as Nick Pappy
the Greek, he becomes finally Nicholas Papadoupalous. Beginning with features of caricature, a comically doleful and self-
tormenting figure with little dimension, he becomes at the end
a man who can look into a human face just for its humanness

and who wonders for the first time where his now-bloated and whining wife had lived when she was a child. Now he has gained the dimension of a character, and personhood in the full sense of the word. So, in their degree, with the other characters who are finally successful—MacCarland Sumpter, for instance, and Monty and Jack Harrick and Timothy Bingham. Not so, however, with those characters who fail—like Isaac Sumpter, Little Ikey—who are forever condemned to be no more than themselves. These retain at the end those features of caricature with which they came onto the scene.

This is what the charge fails to perceive: that here caricature is used deliberately—I assume, deliberately—as a technique. Technique, when successful, reflects idea, or theme, and *The Cave* offers a good example of the way in which this is true. The life trapped in the false self is a stunted life, lacking the full human dimension as caricature lacks the dimension of character. Such a life is, in its way, a caricature of life and invites such a technique as Warren, consciously or unconsciously, has exploited here with brilliance.

A certain stylization is a feature of most Warren novels and *The Cave* is anything but an exception. The technique of caricature described contributes to this feature, as do the deliberate circling structure and the omission of certain kinds of elementary grounding details which a reader looks for in novels more bent on total verisimilitude. The multiplicity of major characters confines the range of their lateral development and hence the staged or theaterlike concentraton of many scenes in which physical gesture and spoken word are the decisive means of rendering character.[5] There is even, so to speak, a center-stage in the novel: that clearing around the cave mouth described in the opening pages, where all the characters eventually gather and which Warren renders in perhaps the finest prose passage he ever wrote. Here the locusts grind and whir, their cry spread-

5. James H. Justus, "The Uses of Gesture in Warren's *The Cave*," *Modern Language Quarterly*, XXVI (1965), 448–61.

ing across the land, asserting itself again and again at strategic moments throughout the novel. "It is easy to forget that it is not from inside you, that glittering, jittering, remorseless whir so much a part of you that you scarcely notice it, and perhaps love it, until the time when you really notice it, and scream." This cry is in fact one of the threads of the novel's unity, drawing us back to the sun-drenched clearing and the dark cave where the man lies trapped.

In its stylization especially, *The Cave* may remind a reader of that masterful though strange novel of Joseph Conrad's, *The Secret Agent*, to which Warren's novel has an interesting technical relationship. So much so, in fact, that one may wonder whether the Conrad novel did not play a part in Warren's original conception. However, in Conrad's novel the stylization is brought to and, I think, beyond its effective limits, maintained by the unrelenting irony of the omniscient narrator's voice. This voice holds us from beginning to end at arm's length from even the novel's most intense emotions. The voice of Warren's omniscient narrator by its irony and detachment sometimes suggests the Conrad voice, but only sometimes. It is not unrelenting and, far from being constant throughout the novel, often vanishes entirely and for long passages is one with the thoughts and feelings of the various characters. The Conrad voice leaves us to make what we will of characters and events. The Warren voice, variously ironic and not ironic, descending and vanishing and rising again, directs our attitudes and, so, interprets as it goes. The stylization of the Conrad novel has an absoluteness that produces finally, for all the author's mastery, a coldness that we do not know quite what to make of. Warren's practice is by comparison partial, flexible, and unobtrusive, a feature rather than veritable backbone of the novel. As such the uniqueness of effect that the stylization contributes does not preclude the kind of legitimate authorial expression needed to shape the reader's attitude toward characters and events.

I said earlier that *The Cave* is the most unique of Warren's novels and tried to indicate why I think this is so. I also said that it is the most human and compassionate of them. The quality of compassion in a novel is so much a matter of tone as to make it hard to illustrate, especially in a brief space. The quality of humanness, though, is a little easier to talk about. In the present case it partly derives from the nature of the characters themselves. More commonly in Warren's novels the important characters, certainly the protagonists, are more or less extremes of troubled humanity, special cases that show us the problem writ large, like the case of Jeremiah Beaumont. In *The Cave* the characters, however provincial, are as recognizable as our neighbors. They include a laborer, a preacher, housewives, a restaurant proprietor, a clerk. One may be reminded of Chaucer's assemblage. The use of characters from humble life does not, of course, by itself produce any special quality in an author's treatment of them. The point here is that the author's theme is dramatized on the level of daily life, its embodiments reduced in scale but not in intensity. Warren's meaning has a special availableness here. It is rendered in terms of trials and griefs and losses that, if not always quite so mundanely typical as our own, move us in much the same way our own troubles do. There is old Jack Harrick, dying of cancer, who, still clinging to that legend of his own great strength, will not take his pill. Not until, through the death of his son in the cave, he is brought to the vision of his own mortal weakness. There is Mac Sumpter, the earnest and upright man of God compelled finally, because he loves his vicious son, to lie, and find the truth. There is Timothy Bingham whose sympathy for his young daughter in her pregnancy moves him at long last to defy his pious harridan of a wife. And there is Celia Harrick, surely the finest of Warren's portraits of women, who through her grief for her son comes to understand what had been false between her husband and herself. So with all the important characters: their personal crises are rendered in terms no less close to home, where husbands and wives and parents and children play the leading roles. The novel works close to the heart of life and this is what gives it its special quality of humanness. And this is a reason, though not the only reason, that *The Cave* stands among the best work of a truly distinguished writer.

Sunset Hawk: Warren's Poetry and Tradition

The beginning is like a god which as long as it dwells among men saves all things.

—Plato, *Laws* 775

Where can an authentic poet begin again, when clearly the past has ceased to throw its illumination upon the future? Robert Penn Warren's poetry spans nearly sixty years, from "Pondy Woods" to his long poem upon Chief Joseph, against whom the United States fought its last serious Indian war. No final perspective is possible upon a strong poet whose own wars are far from over. I have been reading Warren's poetry for thirty years, since I first came to Yale, but only in the second half of that period have I read him with the deep absorption that his poetry demands and rewards. Before the publication of *Incarnations: Poems 1966–1968*, I would have based my judgment of Warren's aesthetic eminence primarily upon his most ambitious novels, *All the King's Men* and *World Enough and Time*. The poetry seemed distinguished, yet overshadowed by Eliot, and perhaps of less intrinsic interest than the best poems of Ransom and Tate. But from *Incarnations* on, without a break, Warren consciously has taken on his full power over language and the world of the senses. In his varied achievement, his poetry now asserts the highest claims upon us.

Incarnations is an extraordinary book, and so it may be arbitrary to single out just one poem, but I still remember the shock with which I first read its strongest poem, "The Leaf." Few moments in the varied history of the American Sublime match Warren's sudden capture of that mode:

59

Near the nesting place of the hawk, among
Snag-rock, high on the cliff, I have seen
The clutter of annual bones of hare, vole, bird, white
As chalk from sun and season, frail
As the dry grass stem. On that

High place of stone I have lain down, the sun
Beat, the small exacerbation
Of dry bones was what my back, shirtless and bare,
    knew. I saw

The hawk shudder in the high sky, he shudders
To hold position in the blazing wind, in relation to
The firmament, he shudders and the world is a metaphor,
    his eye
Sees, white, the flicker of hare-scut, the movement
    of vole.

It may be gratuitous, but I am tempted to find, just here,
a textual point of crossing, the place Warren's poetry turned
about, on his quest for an ultimate strength. Certainly his stance,
style, and thematics are different, in and after this passage
through to the Sublime. "This is the place," Warren had written
earlier in the poem, adding: "To this spot I bring my grief." His
grief, as we might expect from so experiential and dramatic a
writer, doubtless presented itself to him as temporal guilt. But
poetry is a mediated mode of expression, in which poems are
mediated primarily by other poems. I will read Warren's guilt
in "The Leaf" as a literary anxiety, appropriate to a poem's
inescapable dilemma, which is that it must treat literal anguish
as being figurative, in order to find appropriate figuration that
would justify yet another poem. Warren actually may have lain
down on that high place of stone, but the actuality matters only
as another order or degree of trope. "The Leaf" is a crisis poem
of a very traditional kind, and in that kind the crisis concerns
the fate of poetic voice, in a very precise sense of voice. The
sense is American, though the tradition of the crisis poem is
biblical in its origins, and British in its major developments.

Like his poetic father, Eliot, Warren rehearses the crisis poem's origins, but more even than Eliot, Warren develops an acutely American sense of poetic voice. "The Leaf" occupies a place in Warren's canon analogous to the place of *Ash Wednesday* in Eliot's work, but with an American difference necessarily more emphasized in Warren.

Rather than qualify that "necessarily" I would emphasize its double aspect: historical and personal. Both the historical necessity and the personal modification are agonistic. The agon, whether with tradition or with Eliot as tradition's contemporary representative, is ambivalent in Warren, but a loving struggle is not less a struggle. When Warren writes "my tongue / Was like a dry leaf in my mouth," he is writing Eliot's language, and so the tongue still is not quite his own. *Incarnations* has two epigraphs, the first being the opening of Nehemiah 5:5, when the people say to Nehemiah: "Yet now our flesh is as the flesh of our brethren." Warren omits the remainder of the verse, which concludes: "for other men have our lands and our vineyards." The context is the rebuilding of Jerusalem, after the return from exile in Babylon. *Incarnations'* other epigraph is the heroic defiance of John Henry in his ballad: "A man ain't nuthin but a man"—which of course is less an expression of limitation than an assertion of individuality against overwhelming force. The epigraphs point to the secret plot of *Incarnations*, culminating in "The Leaf." Let us call the plot "deferred originality," and with that calling return to everything problematic in the poem. Here is its extraordinary first section:

> Here the fig lets down the leaf, the leaf
> Of the fig five fingers has, the fingers
> Are broad, spatulate, stupid,
> Ill-formed, and innocent—but of a hand, and the hand,
>
> To hide me from the blaze of the wide world, drops,
> Shamefast, down. I am
> What is to be concealed. I lurk

> In the shadow of the fig. Stop.
> Go no further. This is the place.
>
> To this spot I bring my grief.
> Human grief is the obscenity to be hidden by the leaf.

Warren portrays himself as Adam just after the Fall, with partial reference to earlier lyrics about the fig in the first sequence of *Incarnations*, a sequence concluding in "The Leaf." Whether by intuition or by acquired knowledge, Warren seems to have a sense of the ancient Jewish tradition that identified the forbidden fruit with the fig rather than the grape or apple of paradise (*etrog*). Only the fig tree therefore granted Adam permission to take of its leaves when he sought to cover himself. Warren concentrates upon a single leaf, more an emblem or trope of voice than of sexuality. In the second lyric of the "Island of Summer" sequence that closes with the crucial poem called "The Leaf," Warren introduces the trope as a version of death:

> . . . a single
> Leaf the rest screens, but through it, light
> Burns, and for the fig's bliss
> The sun dies . . .

The image of the leaf resumes in the sardonic poem bearing the long and splendid title: "Paul Valéry Stood on the Cliff and Confronted the Furious Energies of Nature." Whether Warren triumphs over the formidable seer of the marine cemetery is perhaps questionable, but we are left with a vivid critique of a transcendental consciousness:

> He sways high against the blue sky,
>   While in the bright intricacies
> Of wind, his mind, like a leaf,
>   Turns. In the sun, it glitters.

Warren would say that this is a disincarnation, and to it he opposes a further lyric in his sequence:

> Where purples now the fig, flame in
> Its inmost flesh, a leaf hangs

Down, and on it, gull-droppings, white
As chalk, show, for the sun has

Burned all white, for the sun, it would
Burn our bones to chalk—yes, keep
Them covered, oh flesh, oh sweet
Integument, oh frail, depart not

And leave me thus exposed, like Truth.

Fig, flame, flesh, leaf, and sun are drawn together here into the dark intricacy that is an incarnation, the truth that is the body of death. With this as prelude, we are ready to return to "The Leaf" as Warren's great poem of the threshold, of a crossing over into his own image of voice. To see how drastic a swerve into originality is made here from the start, we have to recall something of the fiction of the leaves in Western poetry. I've written about this extensively, in *A Map of Misreading* and the more recent *The Breaking of the Vessels*, and don't wish to repeat here the long train of transumptions that holds together the history of this conceptual image from Homer and the Bible through Virgil, Dante, Spenser, and Milton on to Shelley, Whitman, and Wallace Stevens. Warren's fiction of the leaf is a baroque figuration, in a very different tradition. Unlike the transumptive line, Warren does not seek an ellipsis of further figuration. Most simply, Stevens does; Stevens wants the readers of "The Rock" or "The Course of a Particular" to believe that the fiction of the leaves attains a completion in those poems. This is the Romantic and Emersonian credence that Warren refuses, in favor of a more Eliotic vision of tradition and the individual talent. Hence Warren's moral vocabulary of shame and guilt, or should we call it rather his moral refusal to acknowledge that poetry refuses the distinction between shame culture and guilt culture? To refuse that distinction is to attempt an individual closure to tradition; to accept it, as Warren does, is to affirm that one's role is to extend tradition, to hold it open for a community of others. Warren's fundamental postulates, however tempered by skepticism, are biblical and Classical, but his rhetoric and his poetic dilemmas are High Romantic. He thus repeats the fundamental conflicts of his precursor Eliot, whose actual rhetorical art stemmed from Whitman and Tennyson, and not from more baroque sensibilities. Warren's dilemmas in some ways are both simpler and harsher than Eliot's. A shamanistic intensity, a sense of the abruptness of poetic force more suitable to Yeats or Hart Crane than to Eliot, somehow has to be reconciled with a cultural sense that demands rational restraints and the personal acceptance of historical guilt.

The handlike leaf of the fig has fingers that are "broad, spatulate, stupid, / Ill-formed, and innocent," which is pretty well Warren's judgment upon the Adamic condition, a judgment not exactly Emersonian. On what basis are we to accept Warren's peculiarly harsh line: "Human grief is the obscenity to be hidden by the leaf," unless the grief indeed is merely the poet's, any poet's, anxious resentment *as poet* in regard to the almost organic sadness of poetic origins? I am not under the illusion that Warren would accept this reading, but I set aside here my personal reverence for the man and my critical worship of the poet in order to enter again that area of grief that no strong poet will acknowledge as a poet. As I keep discovering, this is not enchanted ground upon which I am driven, doubtless obsessively, to trespass. But I would cite here a touch of external evidence of the most persuasive because most developmental kind. In the decade 1943–1953, when he wrote his most accomplished novels, *All the King's Men* and *World Enough and Time*, Warren's poetry simply stopped. So fecund an imagination does not cease from poetry only because its energies are caught up by the novel. As with Stevens' silence between 1924 and 1934, we have a very problematic gap in a major poetic career, and later in this essay I intend to return to Warren's poetic silence.

In my circular way I have come back to the Sublime second section of "The Leaf," and to the shock of my personal conver-

sion to Warren when I first read the poem in 1969. Ransom and
Tate were poets of enormous talent, but not exactly visionaries
who favored shamanistic symbolic acts in their work, despite
Tate's troubled relation to the primal exuberance of Hart
Crane's poetry. Any close reader of Warren's poetry in 1969
would have known that the flight of hawks meant a great
deal to him, but even that was hardly adequate preparation for
the hawk's shudder in "The Leaf." In Warren's earliest book,
Thirty-Six Poems (1935), there is a remarkable sequence, "Kentucky Mountain Farm," which I continue to hope he will reprint
entire in his next *Selected Poems.* Section VI, "Watershed," not
now available in print, has a memorable and crucially prophetic image: "The sunset hawk now rides / The tall light up the
climbing deep of air." While men sleep, the hawk flies on in the
night, scanning a landscape of disappearances with "gold eyes"
that make all shrivelings reappear. This sunset hawk, first a
vision in boyhood, keeps returning in Warren's poems. In the
still relatively early "To a Friend Parting," the inadequacy of
"the said, the unsaid" is juxtaposed to seeing "The hawk tower,
his wings the light take," an emblem of certainty in pride and
honor. Perhaps it was the absence of such emblems in his confrontation of reality that stopped Warren's poetry in the decade
1943–1953.

Whatever the cause of his silence in verse, it seems significant
that *Promises: Poems 1954–1956* opens with an address to the
poet's infant daughter that culminates in a return of the hawk
image. Viewing the isolated spot to which he has brought his
daughter, Warren celebrates "the hawk-hung delight / Of distance unspoiled and bright space spilled." In *Tale of Time: Poems
1960–1966*, he explicitly compares "hawk shadow" with "that
fugitive thought which I can find no word for," or what we
might call the poetry that would begin anew when he wrote
Incarnations. I quote again the central vision from the second
section of "The Leaf," but extending the quotation now to the
entire section:

We have undergone ourselves, therefore
What more is to be done for Truth's sake? I

Have watched the deployment of ants, I
Have conferred with the flaming mullet in a deep place.

Near the nesting place of the hawk, among
Snag-rock, high on the cliff, I have seen
The clutter of annual bones, of hare, vole, bird, white
As chalk from sun and season, frail
As the dry grass stem. On that

High place of stone I have lain down, the sun
Beat, the small exacerbation
Of dry bones was what my back, shirtless and bare,
        knew. I saw

The hawk shudder in the high sky, he shudders
To hold position in the blazing wind, in relation to
The firmament, he shudders and the world is a metaphor,
        his eye
Sees, white, the flicker of hare-scut, the movement of
        vole.

Distance is nothing, there is no solution, I
Have opened my mouth to the wind of the world like wine,
        I wanted
To taste what the world is, wind dried up

The live saliva of my tongue, my tongue
Was like a dry leaf in my mouth.

Destiny is what you experience, that
Is its name and definition, and is your name, for

The wide world lets down the hand in shame:
Here is the human shadow, there, of the wide world,
        the flame.

The poet offers himself here not to the hawks but to the
hawk's shudder and the hawk's vision, and so to what shudder
and vision incarnate, a stance or holding of position. That
stance casts out shame even as it accepts guilt. That Warren
practices a private ritual is palpable, even though we could only
guess at the ritual until he wrote and published the extraordinary long autobiographical "Red-Tail Hawk and Pyre of Youth"

that is the glory of *Now and Then: Poems 1976–1978*. Although the later poem is finer even than "The Leaf," it is not as pivotal, because it focuses on the young Warren alone, and not on the agon with forebears. What "The Leaf" discovers, with a clarity not often matched in our poetry, is the necessity of mediation despite the poet's longing for an unmediated relation between his mouth and the wind of the world. Both these terms, as Warren well knows, are Shelley's, a poet not much to Warren's taste, and so his treatment of the terms submits them to the stylistic cosmos of Eliot: "wind dried up / The live saliva of my tongue, my tongue / Was like a dry leaf in my mouth." We recognize that this is the Waste Land, and not an Italy waiting for the Revolution. But the revelation that comes is not much more Eliotic than it is Shelleyan:

> The world is fruitful. In this heat
> The plum, black yet bough-bound, bursts, and the gold
>   ooze is,
> Of bees, joy, the gold ooze has striven
> Outward, it wants again to be of
> The goldness of air and—blessèdly—innocent. The grape
> Weakens at the juncture of the stem. The world

> Is fruitful, and I, too,
> In that I am the father
> Of my father's father's father. I,
> Of my father, have set the teeth on edge. But
> By what grape? I have cried out in the night.

> From a further garden, from the shade of another tree,
> My father's voice, in the moment when the
>   cicada
>   ceases, has called to me.

"The moment when the cicada / ceases" deliberately alludes to Eliot's "not the cicada" in "What the Thunder Said"; but the prophetic trope, in its reversal, overcomes the rhetoric of *The Waste Land*. There is a curious ambiguity as to whose is the father's voice that calls out this ambivalent blessing:

> The voice blesses me for the only
> Gift I have given: *teeth set on edge.*
>
> In the momentary silence of the cicada,
> I can hear the appalling speed,
> In space beyond stars, of
> Light. It is
>
> A sound like wind.

It is Warren's gift, by the reversal of the influence process, that has set Eliot's teeth on edge. Which is to say, it is Warren's rhetorical strength to have converted the Eliotic trope of orthodoxy, the light, into the appalling speed that sounds the wind of time, for time is Warren's trope, the center of his poetics. The hawk shudders to hold position in the blazing wind of time, and so transforms the world into a temporal metaphor. Warren's merger of identity with the hawk's shudder affirms the pride of his own stance and theme, the unforgiving shudder of poetic time. I want to hold on to Warren's vision of the hawk in order to trace something of the development of his poetry from *Incarnations* on to this moment. If my procedure is arbitrary, I defend it by the persistence of this vision, or something near to it, throughout his work.

Warren's best volume, *Or Else—Poem/Poems 1968–1974*, ends with an extraordinary poem bearing the curious title, "A Problem in Spatial Composition." The first section composes the space, a sunset through a high window, an eternity that is always beyond, a Sublime from which we are detached, as is traditional. But this is Warren setting us up for his original power in the second section and the closure in a single line of his third:

> [2]
> While out of the green, up-shining ramshackle of leaf,
>   set
> In the lower right foreground, the stub
> Of a great tree, gaunt-blasted and black, thrusts.

> A single
> Arm jags upward, higher goes, and in that perspective,
>   higher
> Than even the dream-blue of distance that is
>   The mountain.
>
>   Then
> Stabs, black, at the infinite saffron of sky.
>
> All is ready.
>
>   The hawk,
> Entering the composition at the upper left frame
> Of the window, glides,
> In the pellucid ease of thought and at
> His breathless angle,
> Down.
>   Breaks speed.
>
>   Hangs with a slight lift and hover.
>
>   Makes contact.
>
> The hawk perches on the topmost, indicative tip of
> The bough's sharp black and skinny jag skyward.
>
> [3]
> The hawk, in an eyeblink, is gone.

This a different kind of hawk's vision, and shall we not call it a deliberate and triumphant figuration for the poet's new style? "The hawk, / . . . glides, / In the pellucid ease of thought and at / His breathless angle, / Down." As the hawk breaks speed and hovers, he "makes contact," giving us a trope that stands, part for whole, for the tense power of Warren's mature art: "The hawk perches on the topmost, indicative tip of / The bough's sharp black and skinny jag skyward." The emphasis is upon the immanent thrust of the natural object, rather than its transcendent possibilities. Another emphasis, as characteristic of Warren, is the temporal swiftness of this fiction of duration, or poem—gone in an eyeblink.

In 1975, Warren wrote a group of poems to form the first

section of his *Selected Poems: 1923–1975*. The second of these poems, "Evening Hawk," is surely one of his dozen or so lyric masterpieces, a culmination of forty years of his art:

> From plane of light to plane, wings dipping through
> Geometries and orchids that the sunset builds,
> Out of the peak's black angularity of shadow, riding
> The last tumultuous avalanche of
> Light above pines and the guttural gorge,
> The hawk comes.
>
> His wing
> Scythes down another day, his motion
> Is that of the honed steel-edge, we hear
> The crashless fall of stalks of Time.
>
> The head of each stalk is heavy with the gold of our error.
>
> Look! look! he is climbing the last light
> Who knows neither Time nor error, and under
> Whose eye, unforgiving, the world, unforgiven, swings
> Into shadow.
>
> Long now,
> The last thrush is still, the last bat
> Now cruises in his sharp hieroglyphics. His wisdom
> Is ancient, too, and immense. The star
> Is steady, like Plato, over the mountain.
>
> If there were no wind we might, we think, hear
> The earth grind on its axis, or history
> Drip in darkness like a leaking pipe in the cellar.

The hawk's motion is that of a scythe reaping time, but Warren has learned more than his distance from the hawk's state of being. I know no single line in him grander than the beautifully oxymoronic "The head of each stalk is heavy with the gold of our error." What is being harvested is our fault, and yet that mistake appears as golden grain. When the poet sublimely cries "Look! look!" to us, I do not hear a Yeatsian exultation, but rather an acceptance of a vision that will forgive us nothing, and yet does not rejoice in that stance. Emerson, Warren once snapped in a now notorious poem, "had forgiven God every-

thing," which is true enough, since Emerson sensibly had forgiven himself everything, and God was identical with what was
oldest in Emerson himself. Warren goes on forgiving God, and
himself, nothing, and implies this is the only way to love God or
the self. One does not imagine Ralph Waldo Emerson invoking
the flight of a hawk as an image of the truth, but the poets of his
tradition—notably Whitman, Stevens, and Hart Crane—have
their own way of coming to terms with such an image. But, to
Emersonians, the hawk is firmly part of Nature, of the Not-Me.
Warren's trespasses upon a near-identity with the hawk clearly
are no part of *that* American tradition.

Warren is not interested in similitudes when he achieves a
Sublime vision, but rather in identifying with some aspect of
the truth, however severely he indicates his own distance from
the truth. I am not much interested in rehearsing Warren's polemic against Emerson because I voted for Emerson a long time
ago, and my love for Warren's poetry is therefore against the
grain. As I wrote once, I read Warren's poetry with a shudder
that is simultaneously spiritual revulsion and total aesthetic
satisfaction, a shudder that only Yeats also evokes for me in this
century.

Much in what is problematic in Warren's hawk poems was
clarified permanently by "Red-Tail Hawk and Pyre of Youth" in
Now and Then, the poem in which Warren himself seems to
have arrived at a full awareness of his creative obsession. Yet the
poem, perhaps at the price of so full a knowing, is in many ways
at variance with Warren's other hawk visions. Beginning with
the boy hunter's confrontation of the hawk's gaze ("Gold eyes,
unforgiving, for they, like God, see all"), Warren moves rapidly
past the miraculous shot to center upon his clay-burlap stuffed
hawk, mounted in his room on a bookshelf of the poets and of
Augustine, set over them as an emblem of the boy's own ambi-
tions. Vividly as this is portrayed, it is less memorable than
Warren's later return to the emblem, and his placing of the
hawk upon a pyre:

8
Flame flared. Feathers first, and I flinched, then stood
As the steel wire warped red to defend
The shape designed godly for air. But
It fell with the mass, and I
Did not wait.

What left
To do but walk in the dark, and no stars?

What is not consumed is the ecstasy of confrontation, the
memory of the encounter shared with the hawk:

9
Some dreams come true, some no.
But I've waked in the night to see
High in the late and uncurdled silver of summer
The pale vortex appear once again—and you come
And always the rifle swings up, though with
The weightlessness now of dream,
The old .30–30 that knows
How to bind us in air-blood and earth-blood together
In our commensurate fate,
Whose name is a name beyond joy.

The vortex is what matters, and part of the point is surely
that the stuffed hawk was merely text, while the vortex was the
truth, the fate beyond joy but also beyond language. Warren's
insistence upon truth puts the value of any fiction, including the
poem he is writing, perhaps too severely into question. It is
hardly possible not to be moved by the final section of "Red-Tail
Hawk and Pyre of Youth," and yet the reader needs an answer to
the query as to just what flared up on that sacrificial pyre:

10
And I pray that in some last dream or delusion,
While hospital wheels creak beneath
And the nurse's soles make their *squeak-squeak* like mice,
I'll again see the first small silvery swirl
Spin outward and downward from sky-height
To bring me the truth in blood-marriage of earth and air—

And all will be as it was
In that paradox of unjoyful joyousness,
Till the dazzling moment when I, a last time, must flinch
From the regally feathered gasoline flare
Of youth's poor, angry, slapdash, and ignorant pyre.

The hawk spins outward and downward not to bring the
truth *as* blood-marriage between boy and bird, but *in* that sac-
rament of slaughter. The killing is not the truth, but only an
angry and youthful way to the truth. What can the truth be
except solipsistic transport, the high and breaking light of the
Sublime? If Warren were Stevens, he might have written, "Am I
that imagine this hawk less satisfied?", but being Warren, he
would deny that he had *imagined* the hawk. Warren longs to be
what Stevens once termed "a hawk of life." Stevens said he
wanted his poems "To meet that hawk's eye and to flinch / Not
at the eye but at the joy of it." Such an ambition stops at similitudes, and shies away from identification. But Warren is about
halfway between the shrewd Stevens and the fanatical Yeats,
whose hawklike hero, Cuchulain, could confront death by crying out, "I make the truth." Like Whitman, Stevens chooses a
fiction that knows itself to be a fiction. Warren, in his prose
"Afterthought" to *Being Here: Poetry 1977–1980*, somberly ends
by remarking that "our lives are our own supreme fiction."
There is an implicit thrust here against Stevens, who would not
have agreed. Yet Warren is a dramatic lyrist, whose boys and
hawks are not fictive. Stevens, infinitely nuanced, would not
have deigned to write a dramatic lyric. In Stevens, "the truth"
sagely reduces to "the the," but Warren wants and needs the
truth, and will risk placing all his own poems and stories upon
the pyre if that will spur the truth to appear.

The risk is extended all through recent Warren, with necessarily mixed results. We are given a poetic art that dares constantly the root meaning of *hamartia*: to shoot wide of the
mark. From the Sublime lyric, this very late Warren has passed

to the tragic mode, which fails sometimes very badly in *Being
Here*, and then suddenly gives us perfection, as in "Eagle
Descending":

> Beyond the last flamed escarpment of mountain cloud
> The eagle rides air currents, switch and swell,
> With spiral upward now, steady as God's will.
>
> Beyond black peak and flaming cloud, he yet
> Stares at the sun—invisible to us,
> Who downward sink. Beyond new ranges, shark-
>
> Toothed, saw-toothed, he stares at the plains afar
> By ghostly shadows eastward combed, and crossed
> By a stream, steel-bright, that seems to have lost its way.
>
> No silly pride of Icarus his! All peril past,
> He westward gazes, and down, where the sun will brush
> The farthermost bulge of earth. How soon? How soon
>
> Will the tangent of his sight now intersect
> The latitudinal curvature where the sun
> Soon crucial contact makes, to leave him in twilight,
>
> Alone in glory? The twilight fades. One wing
> Dips, slow. He leans.—And with that slightest shift,
> Spiral on spiral, mile on mile, uncoils
>
> The wind to sing with joy of truth fulfilled.

This is parenthetically subtitled "To a dead friend," identified
by Warren as Allen Tate, and is an elegy worthy of its subject,
with eagle replacing the personal emblem of the hawk. Hover-
ing throughout, there is a sense of the precursor poem, the first
section of Eliot's *Ash-Wednesday*, a poem equally influential
upon Tate and Warren. The despairing voice that opens *Ash-
Wednesday* has abandoned the agonistic intensities of poetic tradition: "Desiring this man's gift and that man's scope / I no
longer strive to strive towards such things." Warren says of his
eagle that it too has given up the poetic quest if that quest is
only a Sublime battle against human limitations: "No silly
pride of Icarus his!" This eagle's pride is rather in persistence of
sight; he goes on staring at the sun, at the plains of Hades, at

the westward sweep outwards and downwards of human specu-
lation. And this gaze *is* instrumental, for unless it intersects the
sunlight there will not be a final vision "in twilight, / Alone in
glory." That Sublime will survive the fading of twilight, the sur-
vival being manifest in the slow dip of wing with which the
descending eagle makes its last exercise of will. Echoing the
clinamen of Lucretius, Warren celebrates "that slightest shift"
which is poetic and human freedom. Tradition becomes the spiral on spiral, mile on mile, uncoiling of a singing wind whose
message is the fulfilled truth of the eagle's dying will. This does
seem to me a Lucretian rather than a Christian elegy, but so
vexed is the issue of Warren's unforgiving emphasis upon identity of truth and poetry that I express my own judgment here
with considerable qualms.

Warren in his current phase, exemplified by *Rumor Verified:
Poems 1979–1980* and by *Chief Joseph*, still under revision, is in
the midst of undergoing yet another stylistic change, compara-
ble in scope to the one that ensued in *Incarnations* and *Audubon: A Vision*. Clearly he is not one of the poets who unfold,
like Stevens, but one of those who develop, like Yeats. But the
alteration in idiom shows no signs of modifying his obsession
with the identity of poetic truth and the fierce but entropic
freedom emblematic in the image of the hawk. I quote from
Chief Joseph with a gingerly feeling, so revisionary is Warren,
but there is a striking and relevant passage spoken by the chief
as he leads his people's flight from their oppressors:

> Past lava, past schist, past desert and sand—
> A strange land we wandered to eastern horizons
> Where blueness of mountains swam in their blue—
> In blue beyond name. The hawk hung high.
> Gleamed white. A sign. It gleamed like a word in the sky.
> Cleanse hearts and pray. Pray to know what the Sky-Chief
> Would now lean to tell. To the pure heart, Truth speaks.

By now, then, a high-hanging hawk is for Warren not just a
sign, but the inevitable sign of the truth. Nothing is more dan-

gerous for a belated poetry (and as Americans we can have no
other) than to establish a proper sign for the truth. I want to
put Warren's poetry to the test by showing how much that danger both mutilates and enhances his achievement. As a final
exemplary text, I give the final poem of *Now and Then*, "Heart
of Autumn," primarily because I love it best of all Warren's
poems:

> Wind finds the northwest gap, fall comes.
> Today, under gray cloud-scud and over gray
> Wind-flicker of forest, in perfect formation, wild geese
> Head for a land of warm water, the *boom*, the lead pellet.
>
> Some crumple in air, fall. Some stagger, recover control,
> Then take the last glide for a far glint of water. None
> Knows what has happened. Now, today, watching
> How tirelessly *V* upon *V* arrows the season's logic,
>
> Do I know my own story? At least, they know
> When the hour comes for the great wing-beat. Sky-strider,
> Star-rider—they rise, and the imperial utterance,
> Which cries out for distance, quivers in the wheeling sky.
>
> That much they know, and in their nature know
> The path of pathlessness, with all the joy
> Of destiny fulfilling its own name.
> I have known time and distance, but not why I am here.
>
> Path of logic, path of folly, all
> The same—and I stand, my face lifted now skyward,
> Hearing the high beat, my arms outstretched in the tingling
> Process of transformation, and soon tough legs,
>
> With folded feet, trail in the sounding vacuum of passage,
> And my heart is impacted with a fierce impulse
> To unwordable utterance—
> Toward sunset, at a great height.

This seems to me the essential Warren poem, as much his
own invention as "The Course of a Particular" is Stevens' or
"Repose of Rivers" is Hart Crane's. Eliot, prime precursor, is so
repressed here that one might think more readily of Melville or
Hardy—both Shelleyans—as closer to Warren's mode, though

certainly not to his stance or vision. But how much have that stance and vision changed from the poetry of the young Warren? I quote pretty much at random from Warren's earliest verse, and what I hear is the purest Eliot:

> What grief has the mind distilled?
> The heart is unfulfilled
> The hoarse pine stilled
> I cannot pluck
> Out of this land of pine and rock
> Of red bud their season not yet gone
> If I could pluck
> (In drouth the lizard will blink on the hot limestone)
> At the blind hour of unaimed grief,
> Of addition and subtraction,
> Of compromise,
> Of the smoky lecher, the thief,
> Of regretted action,
> At the hour to close the eyes,
> At the hour when lights go out in the houses—
> Then wind rouses
> The kildees from their sodden ground.
> Their commentary is part of the wind's sound.
> What is that other sound,
> Surf or distant cannonade?

Both passages would fit well enough in "Gerontion" or *The Waste Land*, but that was Warren more than a half-century ago. In an older way of critical speaking, you might say that he had weathered Eliot's influence, while extending both Eliot's tradition and Eliot's sense of *the* tradition, the sense we associate with Cleanth Brooks, as with Warren. But I tend to a different kind of critical speaking, one which would emphasize Warren's passage into poetic strength as an agonistic process that the Eliot-Warren-Brooks tradition tends to deprecate, or even to deny. Does a poem like "Heart of Autumn" show Warren in a benign relation to tradition, and does Warren's desire to embody the truth find a place within Eliot's sense of the tradition? Whitman began the final section of *Song of Myself* by juxtaposing himself to the spotted hawk, who swoops by and accuses the poet, complaining "of my gab and my loitering." For the Emersonian Whitman, identification took place not with the hawk, but between one's own empirical and ontological selves. In late Warren, the ontological self is identified with, and as, the flight of wild birds, and "the imperial utterance," crying out for distance, is beyond the human. The "high beat" transforms Warren himself, and he crosses the threshold of a wordless Sublime, as his heart identifies with the heart of autumn. Whatever such an identification is, its vitalism has broken the canons both of Whitman's American Romantic tradition and of Eliot's countertradition of neo-orthodoxy. Warren chooses an identification not available to poets like Whitman, Stevens, and Hart Crane, who know their estrangement from the universe of sense. But his choice of identification also brings to an end Eliot's firm separation between poetry and shamanism. For the tradition of Emerson, Warren feels a range of reaction that varies from genial contempt to puzzled respect. For Eliot's poetry, Warren has the agonistic and ambivalent love that always marks the family romance. A poem like "Heart of Autumn" possesses an extraordinary *ethos*, one that mixes memory and desire, where the memory is of a tradition that clearly could distinguish the path of logic from the path of folly, and the desire is to know the shamanistic path of pathlessness, since the traditional paths have proved to be all the same.

Warren, on this reading, is a sunset hawk at the end of a tradition. His usurpation of the Sublime has about it the aura of a solitary grandeur. "I thirst to know the power and nature of Time . . ." is the Augustinian epigraph of *Being Here*, to which Warren adds: "Time is the dimension in which God strives to define His own being." The epigraph is truer to Warren than the addition is, because the trope of a hawk's shuddering immanence is not wholly appropriate for the God of Abraham, the God of Isaac, the God of Jacob, the God of Jesus. Such a trope, whether in Hopkins or Warren, Yeats or Hart Crane, shows rather the poet's agonistic striving, not so much for the foremost place, but for the blessing of a time without boundaries. In *Audubon*, Warren found the inevitable trope for that time: "They fly / In air that glitters like fluent crystal / And is hard as perfectly transparent iron, they cleave it / With no effort." Such a trope is not an Eliotic baroque extension of tradition, but marks rather an ellipsis of further figuration. Warren stands, his face lifted now skyward, toward sunset, at a great height.

Warren's Poetry: A Reading and Commentary

It is a great honor to do this for my old friend, or, I like to think, in conjunction with my old friend, whose work I admire so greatly and whose friendship and example have been so crucial and so never endingly fruitful for me.

Going back through Red Warren's work, I find that it is all a long, lyric, and dramatic meditation on time, which includes mortality, disease, terror, exultation, death, definition, and meaning or lack of meaning. All writers are obsessed with time, but Warren's preoccupation with it is unique, and takes many forms. It is fascinating to go through his poems and see how many forms he has used and experimented with, and how the preoccupations and the personality remain the same. The personality, as I once said in a review, is tough and mystical. The source of his stunning power is *angst*, a kind of radiant metaphysical terror, projected outward onto the natural world; in his later work particularly into its waiting waste expanses: open field, ocean, desert, mountain range, or the constellations as they feed into the eye a misshapen, baffling, and yearning mythology bred on nothingness.

> So I stood on that knife-edge frontier
> Of Timelessness, knowing that yonder
> Ahead was the life I might live
> Could I but move
> Into the terror of unmarred whiteness under
> The be-nimbed and frozen sun.

As intelligent as he is, Warren's idiom has the feeling usually of something home-crafted. He is a no-nonsense, gut-level kind of poet, and was such even from the beginning when he took part of his idiom from the metaphysical poets, particularly Andrew Marvell.

I am very high on the early Warren as well as the late. I think, as Harold Bloom does, that that part of his work is unduly neglected, especially by Warren himself, and I hope it will be published again or republished so everybody can look at it and see how truly good it is. This one is called "Bearded Oaks." It is about a phenomenon that we in South Carolina and the low country know very well: oaks with Spanish moss that give the landscape an Edgar Allan Poeësque feeling of doom and fate. Warren, lying under the bearded oaks with a belovèd person, abstracts himself and the other person from time. It is as though they were under sea, as though they were built up slowly like part of a coral reef under water. While this timeless moment lasts he can say certain things, remember certain things from the world of time before he has to go back to it. Under the bearded oaks he can see the world of time from the subaqueous perspective and the vantage point that the Spanish moss, the bearded oaks give him and his belovèd.

> The oaks, how subtle and marine,
> Bearded, and all the layered light
> Above them swims; and thus the scene,
> Recessed, awaits the positive night.
>
> So, waiting, we in the grass now lie
> Beneath the languorous tread of light:
> The grasses, kelp-like satisfy
> The nameless motions of the air.
>
> Upon the floor of light, and time,
> Unmurmuring, of polyp made,
> We rest; we are, as light withdraws,
> Twin atolls on a shelf of shade.
>
> Ages to our construction went,
> Dim architecture, hour by hour:
> And violence, forgot now, lent
> The present stillness all its power.

The storm of noon above us rolled
Of light the fury, furious gold,
The long drag troubling us, the depth:
Dark is unrocking, unrippling, still.

Passion and slaughter, ruth, decay
Descend, minutely whispering down
Silted down swaying streams, to lay
Foundation for our voicelessness.

All our debate is voiceless here,
As all our rage, the rage of stone;
If hope is hopeless, then fearless is fear,
And history is thus undone.

Our feet once wrought the hollow street
With echo when the lamps were dead
At windows, once our headlight glare
Disturbed the doe that, leaping, fled.

I do not love you less that now
The caged heart makes iron stroke,
Or less that all that light once gave
The graduate dark should now revoke.

We live in time so little time
And we learn all so painfully,
That we may spare this hour's term
To practice for eternity.

Warren's imagination, however, is not only metaphysical but intensely dramatic—sometimes melodramatic, as the large body of his fiction attests. At its best his dramatic imagination is almost unbearably acute, made more so by his marvelous sense of timing. I refer you to his long poem first published twenty some-odd years ago and then revised a couple of years ago, *Brother to Dragons*, which is in one sense a novel in verse; it concerns a dreadful incident propagated by the two nephews of Thomas Jefferson, the sons of his sister married to a man named Charles Lewis, in Kentucky. The two brothers, Isham and Lilburn, have committed a terrible crime: they have murdered a Negro slave of the family over a trivial incident, an accident in which the slave was involved: the accidental de-

struction of a vase, a keepsake of the mother of the two boys.
Isham and Lilburn took the slave to the meathouse and
chopped him up with an ax. The poem has to do with this
incident and the aftermath of the incident, and the involvement
of Thomas Jefferson, the believer in enlightenment and reason
who must now face this terrible thing in his own family, this
terrible outburst of unreason and violence and crime. I corre-
sponded with Red when he was revising this, and I said, "Whatever you do, don't leave out the part where the night moth—the
night butterfly—comes and lights on Lilburn's finger, after
they've committed the crime." He said, "Oh, no, Jim, I don't
think we're going to. . . . I think I'll leave it out." I said, "Don't
leave it out.—You must not. No, No! The whole poem leads up
to that." It's not a scene of violence, but it has the most terrible
incipient judgment of guilt within it, without *saying* anything
about guilt, without editorializing about guilt, without phi-
losophizing about guilt. This is spoken by Isham, a man in awe
of the violence of his brother Lilburn, who has more or less
instigated this hideous crime. Isham and Lilburn are sitting
alone at night and this happens . . .

> Then in the window, where the dark night was,
> It came a-sudden, but like the stillest breath,
> A big green moth, so big you'd never see,
> The palest green like some ghost leaf alive,
> So big, blown on a breeze you couldn't feel,
> Nor brush your cheek with cool, but it was there.
> Then that big moth, it came so ghost-green by,
> And settled on the paper nigh to Lil.
> Lil looked at it. He looked all steady-slow.
> Then lifted up his hand, so steady and slow,
> The moth, it moved its wings so quiet and slow,
> And Lil kept staring at it waiting there.
> Lil's hand rose up.
>
>   I saw it waiting there.
> The hand I mean, high in the air, and I knew
> That if that hand came down like it could come

So heavy-strong and fast like a painter's paw
And did what it could do, then that would be
The end of something, but durn, I couldn't say
Just what. But just one second, sudden-cold,
I hated Lil. And that was terrible.
I saw the hand up high, and sort of sick
The hate came sudden and I sweated there.
I saw the hand. And then the hand came down.
But not to scare, and touched the table top.
And never stirred. And so my breath came back.

And then that green thing moved, but ne'er a wing.
It crept up slow. It clomb on Lilburn's finger.
The finger never moved. The thing climbed up.
And now the wings all gentle fanned, and slow,
But not to fly, but like it had a mind
To spread and make a show for folks to see,
And the wings moved pale there in the candlelight.
Then slow Lil's hand rose up, up high again.
So high Lil reached, then stopped. It didn't scare.
Not that, but slow it drifted off his hand.
The wing's ne'er moved not much to fan and fly.
It drifted off just like the time had come
To go where it would go, and say good-bye.
And it was gone, and Lil just watched the air.
The thing was gone in the dark outside our door.

Warren's intense concern with love, and with the human beings he loves most, his friends and particularly his family, is
principally one of mystery, fear, and wonder, and of this com-
bination he creates powerful and extraordinary memorable
verse. This is part of a poem to a little girl, aged one year, in a
ruined castle. Warren wrote it after he had not written poems
for many, many years—a period of inactivity that Harold
Bloom was talking about earlier. He lived in Italy, in or near a
ruined fortress about ninety miles north of Rome, he tells me,
and in the poem he speaks of his new child, a little one-year-old
girl. You can see the situation. Here is a ruined fortress, the
ruins of civilization, the ruins of time. You have a natural scene;
you have heat; you have sunlight; you've got this fragile new

little life. And if you put a poet into that . . . with that intensity of scene . . . and that intensity of personal feeling, he's *got* to write! He's got to write or jump off into the sea! Warren, being the poet that he is, *does* write. He breaks his long silence with this poem. This is one of the real dramatic moments of poetry of our time, I think. The poem itself is too long for me to read in its entirety, but I will read the last section, because it brings together so many of Warren's themes. This is the fifth section of the poem called "Colder Fire."

It rained toward day. The morning came sad and white
With silver of sea-sadness and defection of season.
Our joys and convictions are sure, but in that wan light
We moved—your mother and I—in muteness of spirit past
    logical reason.

Now sun, afternoon, and again summer-glitter on sea.
As you to a bright toy, the heart leaps. The heart unlocks
Joy, though we know, shamefaced, the heart's weather should
    not be
Merely a reflex to solstice, or sport of some aggrieved
    equinox.

No, the heart should be steadfast: I know that.
And I sit in the late-sunny lee of the watch-house,
At the fortress point, you on my knee now, and the late
White butterflies over gold thistle conduct their ritual carouse.

In whisperless carnival, in vehemence of gossamer,
Pale ghosts of pale passions of air, the white wings weave.
In tingle and tangle of arabesque, they mount light, pair by
    pair,
As though that tall light were eternal indeed, not merely the
    summer's reprieve.

You leap on my knee, you exclaim at the sun-stung gyration.
And the upper air stirs, as though the vast stillness of sky
Had stirred in its sunlit sleep and made a suspiration,
A luxurious languor of breath, as after love, there is a sigh.

But enough, for the highest sun-scintillant pair are gone
Seaward, past rampart and cliff borne, over blue sea-gleam.

Close to my chair, to a thistle, a butterfly sinks now, flight
 done.
By gold bloom of thistle, white wings pulse under the sky's
 dream.

The sky's dream is enormous, I lift up my eyes.
In sunlight a tatter of mist clings high on the mountain-mass.
The mountain is under the sky, and there the grey scarps rise
Past paths where on their appointed occasions men climb, and
 pass.

Past grain-patch, last apron of vineyard, last terrace of olive,
Past chestnut, past cork grove, where the last carts can go,
Past camp of the charcoal maker, where coals glow in the
 black hive,
The scarps, grey, rise up. Above them is that place I know.

The pines are there, they are large, a deep recess,
Shelf above scarp, enclave of rock, a glade
Benched and withdrawn in the mountain-mass, under the
 peak's duress.
We came there—your mother and I—and rested in that severe
 shade.

Pine-blackness mist-tangled, the peak black above: the glade
 gives
On the empty threshold of air, the hawk-hung delight
Of distance unspooled and bright space spilled—ah, the heart
 thrives!
We stood in that shade and saw sea and land lift in the far
 light.

Now the butterflies dance, time-tattered and disarrayed.
I watch them. I think how above that far scarp's sunlit wall
Mist threads in silence the darkness of boughs, and in that
 shade
Condensed moisture gathers at needle-tip. It glitters, will fall.

I cannot interpret for you this collocation
Of memories. You will live your own life, and contrive
The language of your own heart, but let that conversation,
In the last analysis, be always of whatever truth you would
 live.

For fire flames but in the heart of a colder fire.
All voice is but echo caught from a soundless voice.

Height is not deprivation of valley, nor defect of desire,
But defines, for the fortunate, that joy in which all joys should
   rejoice.

The excruciating mystery of being, and being in time, here
with the other forms of life that are also mortal, is everywhere
in Warren—in fact, it might be said that it *is* Warren, and has
been with him always, as in this description of a migration of
birds he remembers from his boyhood. This poem is very special to me. Years ago, Warren and his wife Eleanor spent a week
with my first wife Maxine and me down on Litchfield Plantation
where we have a condominium arrangement that we've had for
many years and I'm always in despair of making the next pay-
ment on. One of the reasons that we have held on to it was that
occasionally we could invite very special people, friends of ours,
like Red and Eleanor Warren, down to stay with us. That's one
of the most beautiful memories that I have connected with this
place—or indeed with my life in general. I requested this poem
to be read at my wife's funeral six years ago, because it seemed
appropriate. She's buried there under the bearded oaks of
Litchfield Plantation, and it seemed to me that an image from
Warren, to whom she was devoted, was strangely appropriate
for the occasion. We had been all together there. Warren, and
Maxine and myself and Eleanor and we were happy. It seemed
the image of release appropriate to the ceremony. It is the last
part of *Audubon*.

Tell Me a Story
[A]
Long ago, in Kentucky, I, a boy, stood
By a dirt road, in first dark, and heard
The great geese hoot northward.
I could not see them, there being no moon
And the stars sparse. I heard them.

I did not know what was happening in my heart.

It was the season before the elderberry blooms,
Therefore they were going north.

The sound was passing northward.

> [B]

Tell me a story.

In this century, and moment, of mania,
Tell me a story.

Make it a story of great distances, and starlight.

The name of the story will be Time,
But you must not pronounce its name.

Tell me a story of deep delight.

Warren's work has tremendous range, from the utmost darkness to light, beginning in the primal mystery and darkness, in horror, dissolution, excrement, entrails, the fat putridity of death-and-birth, and all the pervasive sexuality and bestial energy that make up the processes of matter and man's own body and arouse in Warren a fascination and loathing, as in this description of a deformed river pirate from his novel *World Enough and Time*. A fascination with the excremental is what you might call metaphysical scatology in Warren, and is one of the most salient things about him. A lot of people will skip over those pages in Warren's novels, and plenty of them in his poetry, too. But they shouldn't, because out of that dark stinking muck comes the light—eventually it *does* come, and is even more terrifying and hard to bear than the darkness. This is the description of the river pirate from his novel *World Enough and Time*:

> He had been spewed up out of the swamps and jungles of Louisiana, or out of some fetid alley of New Orleans—out of that dark and savage swill of bloods—a sort of monstrous bubble that rose to the surface of the pot, of a sort of great brute of the depth that swagged up from the blind, primal mud to reach the light and wallow in the stagnant flood, festooned with algae and the bright slime, with his scaled, armored, horny back just awash, like a log.

Warren is not afraid to look at the muck of death and birth and rebirth, but he can also look full into glory, which is more blinding and perhaps even more terrifying. But he is determined to seek it out and for him it is there—or just may be there, somewhere in the forest, somewhere in memory, somewhere in time.

This is the first version of a poem that he wrote years ago called "Gold Glade." He revised it somewhat and changed the ending, but I prefer the earlier version, which I'll read and finish up what I want to say about Red with this statement of light, rather than with the excremental and enteric darkness that, by means of his remarkable, uncompromising imagination, constitutes the source of light. This is called "Gold Glade."

> Wandering, in autumn, the woods of boyhood,
> Where cedar, black, thick, rode the ridge,
> Heart aimless as rifle, boy-blankness of mood,
> I came where ridge broke, and the great ledge,
> Limestone, set the toe high as treetop by dark edge
>
> Of a gorge, and water hid, grudging and grumbling,
> And I saw, in mind's eye, foam white on
> Wet stone, stone wet-black, white water tumbling,
> And so went down, and with some fright on
> Slick boulders, crossed over. The gorge-depth drew night on,
>
> But high over high rock and leaf-lacing sky
> Showed yet bright and declivity wooed
> My foot by the quietening stream, and so I
> Went on, in quiet, through the beech wood:
> There, in gold light, where the glade gave, it stood.
>
> The glade was geometric, circular, gold,
> No brush or weed breaking that bright gold of leaf-fall.
> In the centre it stood, absolute and bold
> Beyond any heart-hurt, or eye's grief-fall.
> Gold-massy in air, it stood in gold light-fall,
>
> No breathing of air, no leaf now gold-falling,
> No tooth-stitch of squirrel, or any far fox bark,
> No woodpecker coding, or late jay calling.

Silence: gray-shagged, the great shagbark
Gave forth gold light. There could be no dark.

But of course dark came, and I can't recall
What county it was, for the life of me.
Montgomery, Todd, Christian—I know them all.
Was it even Kentucky or Tennessee?
Perhaps just an image that keeps haunting me.

No, no! in no mansion under earth,
Nor imagination's domain of bright air,
But solid in soil that gave it its birth,
It stands, wherever it is, but somewhere.
I shall set my foot, and go there.

Someone has requested . . . some misguided person who
might have been a visiting lecturer . . . suggested that I tail
things off by reading some things of mine, one or two. Should I
do that? I'll read one I wrote and dedicated to Warren. This is
the second part of a poem called "Diabetes," a disease I was
much preoccupied with at the time I wrote this because it inter-
fered with my pleasures. My stance, to use one of Mr. Bloom's
favorite words . . . my stance against time is defiance. This is a
poem about the defiance of one's own mortality and diseases
and fleshly ills. It's also about birds. It's not about hawks, like
Warren's hawks, however; it's about buzzards. If you really look
at buzzards and forget what their function is and forget their
habits, you see that there is not anything in the air that has ever
been more beautiful than a buzzard. Not even a hawk is more
beautiful. This is called "Under Buzzards." This never really
happened; I imagined it to happen. It happened to me, but not
to Warren and me together. If you're a poet, though, you put
yourself wherever you want to be, and you bring in anyone you
like. This is about climbing a hill in north Georgia. The man
here, the poet, the protagonist, has just become aware of his
mortality. He has been told he has diabetes, and that he must
watch out for sugar intake. He's on insulin, but he's also got
some beer with him . . . and *that's* the defiance! The poem ends

on that great climax! But he *thinks*, in his doctor-caused, newly
caused neurosis, that the buzzards have premonitions, and that
they are following *him*! This is called "Under Buzzards," and is
dedicated to Robert Penn Warren.

> Heavy summer. Heavy. Companion, if we climb our mortal
> bodies
>> High with great effort, we shall find ourselves
>>> Flying with the life
>> Of the birds of death. We have come up
>>> Under buzzards   they face us
>
> Slowly   slowly circling   and as we watch them they turn us
>>> Around, and you and I spin
>>> Slowly, slowly rounding
>>> Out the hill. We are level
>> Exactly on this moment: exactly on the same bird-
>
> plane with those deaths. They are the salvation of our sense
>> Of glorious movement. Brother, it is right for us to face
>>> Them every which way, and come to ourselves and
> come
>>> From every direction
>> There is. Whirl and stand fast!
>>> Whence cometh death, O Lord?
>> On the downwind, riding fire,
>
> Of Hogback Ridge.
>>> But listen: what is dead here?
> They are not falling but waiting   but waiting
>>> Riding, and they may know
> The rotten, nervous sweetness of my blood.
>>> Somewhere riding the updraft
> Of a far forest fire, they sense the city sugar
>>> The doctors found in time.
> My eyes are green as lettuce with my diet,
>>> My weight is down,
>
> One pocket nailed with needles and injections, the other
>> dragging
>>> With sugar cubes to balance me in life
>>> And hold my blood
> Level, level. Tell me, black riders, does this do any good?
>> Tell me what I need to know about my time
>>> In the world. O out of the fiery

Furnace of pine-woods, in the sap-smoke and crownfire of
   needles,
      Say when I'll die. When will the sugar rise boiling
            Against me, and my brain be sweetened
            to death?
                  In heavy summer, like this day.
      All right! Physicians, witness! I will shoot my veins
         Full of insulin. Let the needle burn
            In. From your terrible heads
      The flight-blood drains   and you are falling back
            Back to the body-raising

Fire.
      Heavy summer. Heavy. My blood is clear
For a time. Is it too clear? Heat waves are rising
      Without birds. But something is gone from me,
Friend. This is too sensible. Really it is better
      To know when to die   better for my blood
   To stream with the death-wish of birds.
      You know, I had just as soon crush
            This doomed syringe
Between two mountain rocks, and bury this needle in needles

   Of trees. Companion, open that beer.
How the body works   how hard it works
      For its medical books is not
      Everything: everything is how
Much glory is in it: heavy summer is right

For a long drink of beer. Red sugar of my eyeballs
      Feels them turn blindly
In the fire   rising   turning   turning
      Back to Hogback Ridge, and it is all
Delicious, brother: my body is turning   is flashing
   unbalanced
      Sweetness everywhere, and I am calling my birds.

Of Bookish Men and the Fugitives:
A Conversation with Robert Penn Warren

TC: Good Evening. It's been a very cold day here in New Haven, Connecticut, with our guest, Robert Penn Warren, famous American novelist, poet, and critic, three-time winner of the Pulitzer Prize. Mr. Warren, we're sorry you can't be with us at the Southern Studies Institute Program in South Carolina.

RPW: I'm very sorry for more reasons than that of climate— humanly sorry but I must say that our luncheon conversation was some compensation for the fact that I couldn't come.

TC: Well, we'll miss having you there. I would like to ask you first some things about your background as a writer. We're both from the same area of the country; I grew up in Middle Tennessee and you grew up in Todd County, Kentucky, which is really a cultural satellite, I suppose, of Nashville.

RPW: Well, a hundred yards from the state line, whatever you want to call that.

TC: As a matter of fact, you went to high school in Montgomery County, Tennessee, in Clarksville.

RPW: Well, one year. I went the first three years in Guthrie, and being young to graduate from Guthrie was no great feat, I must say. And I couldn't get in Vanderbilt because I was not old enough; so, I had the good sense—or the good luck—to go to a very good high school in Clarksville the next year while waiting for my sixteenth year to go to Vanderbilt. Autobiographically, my family was so bookish. My father read to the children before dinner, or after dinner, poems or history before we had to do our lessons. Every summer from six to fourteen there was a grandfather who was full of quoted poetry and knowledge of American history and Napoleonic campaigns. And never seeing anybody; I would go months without seeing a white boy on the place.

TC: You said you had to memorize a lot.

RPW: That was in school; but of course we know education is in terrible condition. Don't deny that! One thing to be said for the schools in Guthrie, Kentucky, is that you had to memorize poems, good or bad. It's hard to believe it, but in a school of six rooms, twelve grades, and six teachers, I . . . and others . . . read "The White Devil" by John Webster. There was still some contact with literature. It was possible there, in a town like that. And men, the older men, you might say, the better farmers, many of them were men of bookishness.

TC: Do you think being a Kentuckian has had something to do with your approach to the difference between reality and myth? Louis Rubin said something in an essay about you, that more than most writers in Vanderbilt's group in the twenties you had more of a double vision, that you had more of a border-state way of thinking than Faulkner or Eudora Welty, that you never as much subscribed to the myths of the lower South as they did.

RPW: I just don't know . . . I haven't thought about that. I always felt myself more of a Tennesseean than a Kentuckian because . . . only a hundred yards from the state line. . . . And then I lived in Tennessee a lot. I went to college in Tennessee and taught there later on. So I always felt Tennessee . . . I knew it better as a state. I felt it much more my own country than Kentucky. I began to systematically investigate Kentucky later on.

TC: A lot of your work is Kentucky-oriented.

RPW: Yes, but that was just my wanderings in Kentucky. . . . The time I've been wandering in Kentucky, learned Kentucky.

TC: I think another part of that strikes me, another part of that

Kentucky or Tennessee influence on you . . . that border-state
influence is that you were really in the last Confederate generation, weren't you, the last generation of Confederate veterans, people who knew veterans, who heard their tales?

RPW: Well, I spent every summer from age six to fourteen with
a grandfather who had fought in the war. He was also a very
intelligent man, and a bookish man; and he, like my father,
quoted a lot of poetry at the drop of a hat. And he had me
read to him from an old book called *Napoleon and His Mar-
shals*—or he, on the ground, scratched the Battle of Fort Pil-
low or Brice's Crossroads or other adventures and explained
the tactics thereof. So I felt quite Confederate in that sense. It
was purely a literary sense; I felt that that was the way God
had made it.

TC: My great-grandfather rode with Forrest, too; he's the one I
told you deserted after the Battle of Chickamauga. One thing
that strikes me again about that border-state area, Tennessee
and Kentucky, and growing up there, is that even the Confederate army there never indulged in that mythology of the
army of planters' sons, such as the Army of Northern Virginia
has for an image today. It was the rather hard-core western
approach, people very much into evangelical religion—quite
a different image from that of Robert E. Lee's army, wouldn't
you say?

RPW: That picture in general, I think, is right. But also, let's
not forget what was made of the Confederacy by the Civil War
writers who created a mythological Confederacy which has
gained much popularity in the North.

TC: Sometimes it was more popular in the North than in the
South. You went to Vanderbilt when you were sixteen. You
left Guthrie and Clarksville. Was it purely by accident that
Vanderbilt flourished at this time as a cultural center? Wasn't
1914 the big date when the university won control of the
school from the Methodist bishops?

RPW: Sometime along there, before I can remember, anyway.

TC: Then right after that the Fugitive movement started, right before World War I. . . .

RPW: Well, the Fugitive movement had so little to do with Vanderbilt. Certain members of the faculty thought it was rather a shame to be associated with the Fugitive group. It didn't seem good enough academically or something . . . but it started long before my days there. . . . It was before the war, before America got into the war anyway. Some were young businessmen: one was a young banker, one was a merchant . . . young men who were interested in philosophy rather than in poetry who met together because they liked each other, because they all had common interests. That's long before my time. They had all been fighting in the war and then going off to places like Oxford and the Sorbonne . . . as some of these young men did in that period. They got more interested in poetry and Ransom published his first book of poems, just after the war was over. I ran into a man in California, an editor out there, who said: "I know a friend of yours, I have a book of his. . . . He gave it to me the day the first two copies reached him in France." And he had the second copy. So this book came out during or just after the war when Ransom was still in uniform.

TC: Was that *Poems About God*?

RPW: That's right. Ransom, as I remember was an officer of regulars—Davidson of volunteers. They had very different attitudes toward the war. Ransom rarely mentioned it and certainly had no romantic view of war. He was the old twenty-year man, you know. He was in artillery. But there was something of a romantic spirit of war about Davidson. I once started out to be a naval officer. I had an appointment to Annapolis and couldn't go because of an accident. But my desire was to be admiral of the Pacific Fleet of course. . . . Who wouldn't want to be admiral of the Pacific Fleet? I could clearly tell there was going to be a war with Japan—but I was saved from the burning.

TC: After World War I, you were sixteen when you entered Vanderbilt in 1921 and became a member of the Fugitive group.

RPW: I entered college in '21 so it must have been '23. I'm guessing now. I can't be sure. . . .

TC: My impression is the Fugitives had really kind of divided into two groups: those who took it seriously as a poetic exercise, like yourself and Ransom or Allen Tate, and some local businessmen whom you could almost call dilettantes.

RPW: Well, they were serious in their thinking about it. Some of those men were clearly not poets . . . were not talented the way Ransom was, but they were serious about their interest and they would talk seriously. They could understand what was going on; they had opinions that were argued. I remember that quite well.

TC: You roomed with Allen Tate at the old Theological School.

RPW: Well, when I was a freshman, the only undergraduate was a man named Ridley Wills who had been in the army in the Tennessee regiment that Luke Lea commanded.

TC: The one that tried to capture the Kaiser.

RPW: Tried to capture the Kaiser. Ridley had come back to finish his degree . . . and I was seeing a young man, an undergraduate who had written a real book published by a real New York publishing house. I thought that was quite wonderful, and it *is* quite wonderful when you are sixteen to have a friend like that. And he asked me to come room with him and he was rather a wag . . . a very funny man . . . a very great wit and so he said: "I'm getting a room over in the Theological Dormitory," which was a piece of early Methodist Gothic, about five stories high. And so we got a room over there among the theologs, as a kind of joke we were playing on ourselves. And then, the next thing he brought in Allen. It was a little bitty room and two double-decker beds. Allen took one of the double-decker beds. And then another came in and there were four of us. In the evenings among the dirty sheets and cigarette butts and not-quite-dry bottles in the corners, poetry was discussed and argued and so was modern philosophy. Tate and Wills were much older than the others and dominated. This became a kind of nameless club. Most people were undergraduates, but they led a very active undergraduate literary life . . . had the last of an old-fashioned kind of teaching in some of the classes. In freshman English you had to memorize at least nine hundred lines of Tennyson before Christmas and be tested on it. You had to memorize things.

TC: Did you memorize Coleridge?

RPW: Not then, no. I found I could memorize poetry very easily because I had been living with it all my life with my father and my grandfather and so I enjoyed doing it. Many students would line up just to buy the latest *New Republic* to see the latest poem by Yeats or Frost that might be in there. There was a large, a big interest among the undergraduates. It is very hard to understand now in my later years of teaching, the lack of that, by and large, in the undergraduate body.

TC: So you say, Mr. Warren, that there were really two poetry groups at Vanderbilt?

RPW: Two, quite different. One was undergraduate and this poetry club met regularly, wrote a great deal, published a book, a hard cover book of their own, before *The Fugitive*—or just after *The Fugitive* began to come out. Just after, I guess. The poetry of Eliot, particularly *The Waste Land*, had a tremendous impact. You could probably find twenty people who could quote it in the freshman and sophomore classes. This sounds romantic but it wasn't. There was a sense that this was new; something was happening or was felt to be happening. And there was! An interpenetration of the young students and people like Wills and Tate who were older, who were members of the Fugitive group through this room that I mentioned where Tate and I lived. You see, it was kind of an interrelationship and this was something I haven't seen duplicated—this passionate interest in an art or in certain ideas that occurred then. And later on, being personal: when I was

struggling with my poems, Wills and Tate would come in; and
I might be asleep; and they would sit down and start revising
them or talk to me the next day about them . . . or criticize.
So I was getting a kind of tutorial free during that period. But
I was not alone. There were a lot of young men in the same
situation, only I was more privileged by having these guard-
ians, as it were, at hand.

TC: A lot of people who have written on you—as you well know
there's a book of 275 pages which is nothing more than a
bibliography of writing that you have done and a bibliography
of things people have written about you. And a lot of people
have commented on John Crowe Ransom's influence on you at
this time—that there was a tremendous influence in two re-
spects: one was in the nature of a poem. . . . Did he teach you
something about what a poem was supposed to be?

RPW: He taught it to everybody who would listen! In his class
he always brought a new angle, a new view to the question of
a poem and explained its especial qualities. Never, ever as a
job, but always as a kind of running comment. And his influence on a lot of people—and many people have said this—
was highly personal. That is, it was not the question of what
he had to say or what he had in his head, but a kind of personal dignity and personal self-control that was felt by almost
everybody around him; and he was a man who was greatly
full of fun and loved poker and loved athletic activity.

TC: He almost believed that a poem was a miniature world,
didn't he, an entity of interplay complete with a backdrop
and landscape?

RPW: I remember one thing when I saw his first book when I
was a freshman. There's a man who's written a book. That
was a great shock. There stands that little man who has written that book. And I read the book; and the book was mostly
about the background that I knew. It was about the background of Tennessee, Kentucky, and north Mississippi, you
see. And he somehow brought poetry into your world, my

world. You felt it was a world that you inhabited. Now that
book is not anything like his real books that came later, but it
did bring the sense of poetry belonging to life, poetry being
connected with life—with your life, your place. I remember
that very strongly and the effect it had on me. . . . Later on I
heard him say, "I want to be a domestic poet. I want to write
about the small things of life as I live it." And you can see that
in his poetry. Well, I must say that wasn't exactly my ambition . . . or the ambition of say, Allen Tate, but the perfection
of Ransom, he was a perfectionist. His small poems are perfectly done . . . perfectly done, and of deep feeling. . . .

TC: Did he influence you a lot in your later approach to the
New Criticism, and attention to text, to images?

RPW: He always did. Later on it became more formalized. But
he was constantly, from the time of the freshman class on.
Mimms taught the poetry one day a week. Two days a week
Ransom taught the writing; and the writing meant all sort of
stylistic problems brought to the level that a freshman could
understand. After the first term (I boast now a little bit), he
said, "I'm taking you out of my class, I'm taking you to another class I have which is more concerned with the problems
I'm now dealing with." And this was the greatest day of my
life. That he would then give *me* some personal attention in
another class of older people.

TC: I believe, in 1930, came *God Without Thunder* in which
Ransom defended belief in religion; and he said in effect that
religion was almost a metaphysical myth established in order
to understand nature. One thing I've noticed about those
of you gathered at Vanderbilt in that day is that most of
you came out of that common heritage of Middle Tennessee, southern Kentucky evangelical religion: Methodist/
Baptist. . . .

RPW: I came out of it with no religion at all. My father was
called an old-fashioned free thinker who gave me Darwin to

read when I was fourteen. He also made me read the Bible.
. . . He played fair.

TC: But, don't you think as a group that religion, that southern
religion in the upper South did affect their whole view of
being somewhere between the Old South, the agrarian South
that had passed and the industrial New South?

RPW: I think it may have had. Now let me tell you one thing
about Ransom in *God Without Thunder*. In the end, that book
is not a book about religion at all. It is a philosophical work.
Because, really, it just dawned on me that that's what the
book's about, not a theological book at all. Way back in 1931,
standing in a kitchen, with a bottle of bourbon in hand, pour-
ing me a drink, he said: "I find it very odd that I who am not
a religious man, should write such a book; but I had to write
it for the truth that's in it." Now he said that to me in '31 and
it clarified something in my mind about it, myself being a
very nonreligious man . . . not antireligious; that is, I have
the deepest awareness of its importance. But I'm a yearner. I
mean I wish I were religious. Ransom certainly said that
religion is a necessary myth; a necessary myth is what he was
saying—to paraphrase him. You see what I'm trying to say?
I'm bumbling it I'm sure.

TC: In one form or another did not a lot of people in the Vanderbilt group in the twenties, some of whom were later in the
Agrarian group, cope with religion? Allen Tate, for example,
coped with religion in a different way.

RPW: He was deeply concerned. He was a Catholic twice! And
buried a Catholic.

TC: Your own approach wasn't a total rejection was it? You
talked sometimes of what you said was a "religious sense" in
your work. You've mentioned that several times.

RPW: I think it is. It's about the quest for religion.

TC: After graduating you went to California and then went to
graduate school and became in a sense, a non-southerner.

How important do you think it is in your own writing that you had a quality of what you would call alienation, being out of the South?

RPW: May I interrupt just a second? I think I became a southerner by going to California and to Connecticut and New England. When I was at Vanderbilt, I couldn't have been paid to go to the Scopes trial. I was right there by it. I was not concerned with it, at all. My Civil War was primarily anecdotal from my acquaintance with old soldiers. They were my old soldiers all right. When I went west I began to read, much more than in some of the graduate courses I had, southern history and American history. That continued. I really became a southerner by not being there.

TC: Do you think southerners sometimes have a love/hate relationship with the South?

RPW: Well, I think that is necessary, there's so much wrong with it and there's so much right with it. You have to have it divided. I was always not at ease with the whole race question and I wrote two books about it.

TC: *Segregation. . . .*

RPW: . . . and then the other one [*Who Speaks for the Negro?*]. Previously, the Agrarian thing was an essay about it. . . . It was a constant nag to me.

TC: In your book *Segregation*, which is subtitled *The Inner Conflict*, you talk about the race problem as being one you called "self-division," not just division of a society between a southerner and society but the self-division within a man.

RPW: One woman, an extremely intelligent woman and a thoughtful woman, a well-educated woman, talking about this to me during the period that I was writing that book, said (she was a religious woman, too, in a very intelligent way, not just automatically so), "I pray to God to change some of my feelings about this question." Now she was really divided.

TC: As long as we're on this subject, may I ask you this? When the Agrarian movement came along—and I know that your relationship to the Vanderbilt Agrarians is quite different from many of them—that you were far less into the economic and political interests. But you received some criticism for your essay "The Briar Patch."

RPW: Are you referring to criticism from my friends or others? I got both kinds!

TC: I was referring to criticism from others, that from a position standpoint they felt that your essay was attempting to defend a racial status quo.

RPW: I was just very uncomfortable with the piece, but it was this. My position was exactly that of the Supreme Court. Equal, you see; "different but equal" was the view of the Supreme Court and of 99 percent of the white people in the country.

TC: You feel very strongly about that criticism of the thirties.

RPW: Well, I think that point is quite clear. Unless I misremember the book entirely—and I haven't read it in a thousand years and don't intend to read it again—that was the basic legal view of the world and that was the one I took. Now that doesn't cover the whole case. There are all sorts of things gone and done and there was unevenness of all kinds. But I remember this quite distinctly that my father, who was a very remarkable man in many ways, saying to me when I made some slurring remark about a Negro, he said: "I have never found a man whom I have treated like a decent human being that has not treated me like one." Another time, using the word "nigger" in his presence. . . . "Never let me hear that word come out of your lips again!" These things I just told you occurred when I was ten or twelve, something like that. But the other part . . . equal pay/equal work, that's clear enough in there. And the Supreme Court view of equal schools and equality . . . but a social difference . . . a social distinction between them . . . a separation. And that's about all of that! Now the way I came back after many years away from the South . . . to live in the South in 1930. . . .

TC: When you came back to Vanderbilt?

RPW: I came back to Memphis first, to Southwestern College. I was then struck by the quite undefinable pressures that were there. It didn't come under the picture I had remembered. I felt quite differently and bit by bit it crept into my poetry. Vinegar Hill was the name of a Negro graveyard in Todd County. And some others. There's something about a lynching in "Pondy Woods." It is something that has always been on my mind in some way or another. There was some sort of confusion of mind about it. Then in novels later on, it began to enter in. *Band of Angels* is such a book, a novel about that question primarily and what it means to be free. You can be enslaved in many ways, the book says. What does it mean to be free . . . the book's about that. Then there are the two books directly on the subject which I did first for *Life* magazine and the second for *Look* magazine. *Segregation* was done originally for *Life*. The other was done originally as an option for parts of it for *Look*. I had to have somebody to pay the bills. I was taking two years off, you see, to make a living. They would pick up the bills.

TC: I think one of the ironies of the criticism you received for "The Briar Patch" is that it was almost your only effort for the Agrarians. And yet, so many times people have identified you with the Vanderbilt Agrarians, but weren't you really a lot different?

RPW: "Agrarianism" is just a word. It did not describe in any basic fashion to my mind what the thing was about. It was like a tent with a menagerie, with fifty kinds of animals under it. Disagreement was more important than agreement. Now for instance, in the industrialized, mechanized world, a man like Ransom would feel, I think, primarily that other things, too, are involved here, not only economic problems, but would also feel that this is a misunderstanding of man's relationship to nature . . . using nature as a thing to be exploited, as a tool of man and not as man having a relationship to nature which is both aesthetic and spiritual. See what I'm driving at? I think his emphasis was going somewhere in that direction and mine would have gone somewhere in that direction, too.

TC: But not Donald Davidson?

RPW: Not Donald Davidson! In many ways, he was like those people who see the violation of nature as a way to commit suicide, for society to commit suicide. Then there are the people who really took it as a way to go live, like Andrew Lytle's buying a farm, and running a farm and trying to be a writer at the same time! Well, you can be a writer at the same time if you don't write very much! I know enough about farming to know it takes time. I would never have tried . . . I like to live in the country. I do live in the country. I have a place in the country in Vermont and I have a place in the country in Connecticut.

TC: The land was more of a metaphor for you wasn't it?

RPW: That was the place to be alone. A year's time in the city is enough for me. I have been in many cities but that's enough. I want to see myself in relation to the natural objects. That is an important point in my life and I basically live in the country. I go to the city and I've lived in many cities. I've lived in San Francisco a long time and then New York and Rome and other cities . . . Paris, and London . . . but I don't stay there.

TC: One thing I've noticed . . . one difference between you and the other Agrarians is the way you deal with history. That you were never that concerned with the events, rather what you called the historical sense, the meaning of the event, the philosophy of the event. I've seen that even in your poetry. I brought one of your poems which I wish you would read for the audience. It's from "Kentucky Mountain Farm." It's "History Among the Rocks."

RPW: This is so long ago. I'm turning now back to my twenties. I'm glad it's not a mirror. This is also a poem that involves, you might say, the divided world of the Confederacy, of the

Civil War. And I was thinking specifically here of a division of the hill sections of Kentucky—which these sections of Kentucky were, then completely unknown to me firsthand. This was purely just fact I knew from other sources. I had never been in the Kentucky mountains until I was a grown man, quite grown.

History Among the Rocks

There are many ways to die
Here among the rocks in any weather;
Wind down the eastern gap, will lie
Level along the snow, beating the cedar,
And lull the drowsy head that it blows over
To startle a cold and crystalline dream forever.

The hound's black paw will print the grass in May,
And sycamores rise down a dark ravine,
Where a creek in flood, sucking the rock and clay,
Will tumble the laurel, the sycamore away.
Think how a body, naked and lean
And white as the splintered sycamore, would go
Tumbling and turning, hushed in the end,
With hair afloat in waters that gently bend
To ocean where the blind tides flow.

Under the shadow of ripe wheat,
By flat limestone, will coil the copperhead,
Fanged as the sunlight, hearing the reaper's feet.
But there are other ways, the lean men said:
In these autumn orchards once young men lay dead—
Gray coats, blue coats. Young men on the mountainside
Clambered, fought. Heels muddied the rocky spring.
Their reason is hard to guess, remembering
Blood on their black mustaches in moonlight.
Their reason is hard to guess and a long time past:
The apple falls, falling in the quiet night.

TC: Someone said about you that you are not a historical poet, historical novelist, but that you are a philosophical poet and novelist who uses history for understanding. History permeates so much of your poetry . . . and your fiction, of course.

RPW: I don't see a sharp division between the use of history in the two things. I can see what they mean by saying that. Looking back on the origins of one thing, a poem, another thing a novel, I see something very similar, not basically different. Now the poetry tends to be more philosophical because it's less narrative. It has only an echo of narrative in it. Most poetry does.

TC: Your use of history is not just facts; it's symbols, really.

RPW: It is the significance of those facts.

TC: Do you think a poet or a novelist, I always thought so, in some ways can be a better historian than a historian? That he can generalize about. . . .

RPW: Well, he might be. . . . Which historian?

TC: This idea of tension in history, of tension between the past and the present certainly permeates at least the first five of your novels.

RPW: Novel after novel that I have written, and poem after poem, have had some germ in historical reality. I mean it had some germ in it. It's interpreting that not as mere history, but as history moralized, to use a more obvious word.

TC: I know in your first five novels you had this common theme of a search for understanding and this kind of tension between the ideal and the practical—of a self-division within a person as he gropes for understanding in reaching back to the past. I got the impression when I read *The Legacy of the Civil War* that you were taking the same structure and applying it to the nation as a whole.

RPW: Well, I wouldn't deny that. I wouldn't know how to deny that, really. I think I see what you mean more clearly now.

TC: Do you think the Civil War was the great southern experience, the great catalyst?

RPW: Well, it's the thing that we most violently lived through as a nation. It also produced our power. And I'm glad of our power, but I think there is also a great danger in the kind of victory that was had. We have been lulled into the assumption that the mechanical expert and the advertising man can control all the values of life. I can't quite bring myself to believe that.

TC: And I think in sixty years of writing, in your poems and your criticism and your fiction, that you never have believed that.

RPW: I never have.

TC: Mr. Warren, I want to thank you for giving us this interview and again we regret that you can't be with us at the Institute for Southern Studies at the University of South Carolina.

RPW: I regret it deeply for personal reasons, not that I regret I can't bring the wisdom fresh off the griddle, but I regret not seeing your human presences before me.

Notes on Contributors

HAROLD BLOOM, university professor in the humanities at Yale, received his Ph.D. from Yale and has honorary degrees from Boston College and Yeshiva University. Among his awards are the prestigious John Addison Porter Prize (1956) and the Melville Cane Award of the Poetry Society of America (1971). He is the author of numerous publications including *Yeats* (Oxford, 1970), *The Visionary Company* (Cornell, rev. ed., 1971), *The Anxiety of Influence* (Oxford, 1973), *Poetry and Repression* (Yale, 1977), *Wallace Stevens: The Poems of Our Climate* (Cornell, 1977), and *Agon* (Oxford, 1982).

THOMAS L. CONNELLY, professor of history at the University of South Carolina, received his Ph.D. from Rice University. He has received a number of awards, including the Jules Landry Award (1971), the Fletcher Pratt Award (1972), and two Jefferson Davis awards (1972 and 1974)—all for his writings on southern and Civil War history. His publications include *Army of the Heartland* (LSU, 1967), *Autumn of Glory* (LSU, 1971), *The Politics of Command* (LSU, 1973), *The Marble Man: Robert E. Lee and His Image in American Society* (Knopf, 1977), *Civil War Tennessee* (Tennessee, 1979), and *Will Campbell and the Soul of the South* (Seabury, 1982).

JAMES DICKEY, professor of English and poet in residence at the University of South Carolina, received his undergraduate and graduate training at Vanderbilt University. In 1966 he won the National Book Award for Poetry for *Buckdancer's Choice*.

111

Among his other works are *The Eyebeaters* (Doubleday, 1970), *Self-Interviews* (Doubleday, 1970), *Deliverance* (Houghton Mifflin, 1970), *Jericho* (Oxmoor, 1977), and *Babel to Byzantium* (Ecco, 1981).

WALTER B. EDGAR, director of the Institute for Southern Studies and professor of history at the University of South Carolina, received his A.B. from Davidson College and his Ph.D. from the University of South Carolina. He has been active in the applied history movement and was the founder and first director of South Carolina's highly successful program.

MADISON JONES, professor of English and writer in residence at Auburn University, studied at Vanderbilt and at the University of Florida. His first novel, *The Innocent*, was published in 1957. Since then, he has authored six others: *Forest of the Night* (Harcourt, 1960), *A Buried Land* (Viking, 1963), *An Exile* (Viking, 1967), *A Cry of Absence* (Crown, 1971), *Passage Through Gehenna* (LSU, 1978), and *Season of the Strangler* (Doubleday, 1982).

LOUIS D. RUBIN, JR., Distinguished Professor of English at the University of North Carolina, received his Ph.D. from Johns Hopkins University. He is the author of a wide range of books, including *The Faraway Country* (Washington, 1963), *The Teller of the Tale* (Washington, 1967), *The Curious Death of the Novel and Other Essays* (LSU, 1967), *George W. Cable* (Pegasus, 1969), *The Writer in the South* (Georgia, 1972), *William Elliott Shoots a Bear* (LSU, 1975), and *The Surfaces of a Diamond* (LSU, 1981).

Index

Eliot, George, 50
Eliot, T. S., 13, 23, 27, 31, 59, 63, 64, 67–68, 76–78, 100; politics *vs.* poetry of, 28; *Ash-Wednesday*, 61, 74
Emerson, Ralph Waldo, 4, 63, 78; Warren on, 70–71. *See also* Transcendentalism
"Evening Hawk," 70–71

Father: in Warren's writings generally, 4, 5, 9–10, 67–68; of Warren, 8, 95–96; of Jack Burden, 44; surrogate of Jeremiah Beaumont, 48
Faulkner, William, 15, 23–24, 35, 40, 96
Flaws in Warren's work, 36, 40–46, 51; *All the King's Men*, 43–45; *Band of Angels*, 45–46. *See also* Risks of failure in Warren's poetry
Formalism, 35
French literary criticism, 29. *See also* Barthes, Roland
Frost, Robert, 32, 34
The Fugitive, 11
Fugitive Group, 10, 11, 12–14, 98–99

Generations, literary, 29. *See also* Vanderbilt University
"Gold Glade," 90–91
Gold, Mike, 25
Graduate studies, 10, 13, 14
Grandfather of Warren, 7–9, 17, 96, 97
Graveyards, 3, 4, 11, 106
Great Confederate Novel, 17
"'The Great Mirage': Conrad and *Nostromo*," 6, 23, 36. *See also* Conrad, Joseph
Guilt, 60, 63–64, 66, 70, 84

Hardy, Thomas, 76
Hartman, Geoffrey, 27
"Harvard '61: Battle of Fatigue," 3
Hawkes, Terence, 22–25
Hawks and eagles, 60, 65–79
Hawthorne, Nathaniel, 4, 40
"Heart of Autumn," 76–77, 78
Hemingway, Ernest, 24
Hicks, Granville, 25

History: southern view of, 9; in Warren's works generally, 30, 108–109; *World Enough and Time*, 46–49; "Eveninng Hawk," 70. *See also* Guilt; Themes of Warren's work
"History Among the Rocks," 3, 107–108
History *vs.* poetry, 2, 5
Hobbes, Thomas, 13
Honors and prizes, 1, 95. *See also* Reception of Warren's work

Idiom of Warren, 81–82
I'll Take My Stand: The South and the Agrarian Tradition, 13
Incarnation: Poems 1966–1968, 59, 61, 75. *See also* "The Leaf"; "Paul Valéry"

John Brown: The Making of a Martyr, 1, 3, 7, 15
Justus, James H., 35–36

Kentucky, 7–8, 96
"Kentucky Mountain Farm," 10, 65, 107. *See also* "History Among the Rocks"

"The Leaf," 59–67
Leaves, 61–63
The Legacy of the Civil War, 16, 109
Lewis, Lucy, 6, 83
Literary criticism by Warren, 29; purpose, 19; examples, 23–24, 28, 32; method, 30–32, 35; influence, 30–31. *See also* New Criticism
Literary generations, 29. *See also* Vanderbilt University
"Literature as a Symptom," 14
Lost Cause, 16–17
Lytle, Andrew, 107

Marvell, Andrew, 82
Marxist critique of New Criticism, 22–25, 27
Meet Me in the Green Glen, 46
Melville, Herman, 32, 33, 34, 35, 76
Metaphysical poets, 31–32, 82